NATIONAL GEOGRAPHIC
KiDS

Bet you didn't know!

Fascinating, Far-out, Fun-tastic Facts

NATIONAL GEOGRAPHIC
WASHINGTON, D.C.

Contents

6 Stellar Facts About Stars

8 Mouthwatering Facts About Ice Cream

10 Epic Facts About Mythology

12 Bite-Size Facts About Dinosaurs

14 What's the Difference?

16 Wacky Facts About Weather

18 Incredibly Odd Laws in the U.S.A.

20 Bold Facts to Color Your World

24 Fantastic Facts About Families

26 Fiery Facts About Dragons

28 Facts That Are Too Hot to Handle

30 One Monstrous Fact About Dinosaurs

32 Megacool Facts About Mars

34 Bizarre Facts About the Human Body

38 Money Facts You Can Bank On

40 Wild Facts About Animals

42 Strange Places: "Ice" Castle

44 Fetching Facts About Canines

46 Page-Turning Facts About Books

48 Food Facts to Drool Over

52 Frosty Facts About Snow

54 Extreme Weirdness

56 Uplifting Facts About Flight

58 Fortunate Facts About Luck

62 Vibrant Facts About the Color Red

64 Wonderful Facts About the World

66 Sweet Facts About Chocolate

68 What's the Difference?

70 Facts About Leaders Who Rule

72 Riveting Facts About Rain Forests

74 Facts of Amazing Proportion

76 Sweet Facts About Desserts

78 Incredible Facts About Your Impact on the World

80 One Radical Fact About the Color Red

82 Heart Facts to Get You Pumped

84 Mummy Facts to Unwrap

86 Stunning Facts About Science

88 Marvelous Marsupials

90 Amazing Facts About the Ancient World

92 Out-of-This-World Facts About Space

94 Strange Places: Secrets of a Stone City

96 Crazy Facts About Creepy-Crawlies

98 Priceless Facts About Treasures

100 Earthshaking Facts About Geology

Bet you
didn't
know!

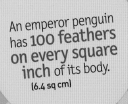

An emperor penguin
has **100 feathers**
on every square
inch of its body.
(6.4 sq cm)

102 Bee Facts to Buzz About

104 Fun Facts to Unwrap About Winter Holidays

106 Extreme Weirdness

108 Deep Facts About Caves

110 Frrr-ozen Facts to Chill You Out

112 Rad Facts About Rodents

114 Snazzy Facts About Sea Creatures

116 Facts About Daring Dining

118 Record-Breakers That Rock

120 Facts You Can Count On

122 Astounding Facts About Africa

124 Surprising Facts About Sharks

126 What's the Difference?

128 Stately Facts About U.S. Presidents

130 Facts About Wild Cats That Are Claw-Some

132 Cool Facts About Castles

134 One Heart-Stopping Fact About Blue Whales

136 Icky Facts to Creep You Out

138 Facts to Light Up Your World

140 Awesome Facts About Animals in the Americas

142 Strange Places: City in the Sky

144 Purr-fect Facts About Cats

146 Surprising Facts About Spiders

148 Splashy Facts to Dive Into!

150 Fab Facts About Bats

152 Festive Facts About Holidays Around the World

154 Facts to Bug You Out

156 Extreme Weirdness

158 Halloween Facts to Howl About

160 Listen Up for These Facts About Sound

162 What's the Difference?

164 Dolphin Facts to Flip Over

166 Ultracool Facts About the Unseen World

168 Facts About Plants to Grow Your Brain

170 Mind-Bending Facts About the Brain

172 Antarctic Facts That Will Give You the Chills

174 One Sticky Fact About Sea Cucumbers

176 Sense-ational Facts

178 Frog Facts to Jump Into!

180 Incredible Facts About Ancient Egypt

182 Behind the Facts

182 Illustrations Credits

184 Index

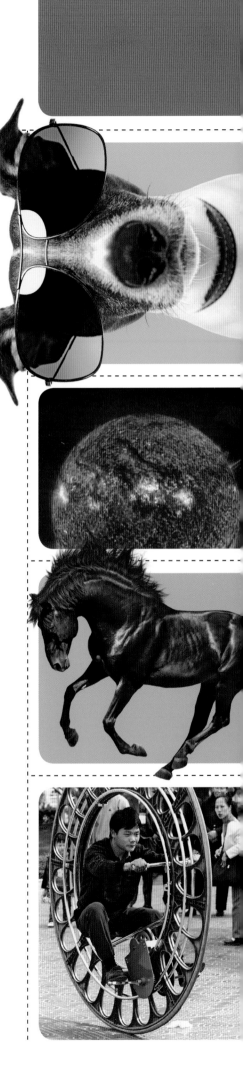

1

Our galaxy, known as the **Milky Way,** contains an estimated **200 to 400 billion stars.**

2

The fastest **spinning star** ever **discovered, VFTS 102,** rotates at a **million miles an hour** (1.6 million km/h).

3

A **"zombie star"** is a surviving fragment of a star that **exploded.**

4

Scientists have **created** pieces of **white dwarf stars** in a lab.

5

Harry Potter characters **Sirius Black** and **Bellatrix Lestrange** were named after **stars.**

6

Constellations named in the year **1754** that didn't catch on include **Limax** the slug, **Anguilla** the eel, **Bufo** the toad, and **Scarabaeus** the rhinoceros beetle.

Stellar
Facts About
Stars

7

The star **VY Canis Majoris** is so large, a **plane would take** more than a **thousand years** to orbit it.

8

The **light** you see from stars is actually light that **left the star millions of years ago—** that's how long it takes to **reach the Earth.**

9

A **blue bird** called the **indigo bunting** migrates at night, using the stars to **navigate.**

10

A **teaspoon** of neutron star material weighs about **10 million tons** (9.1 million t)—— that's about the same as **44,444 Statues of Liberty.**

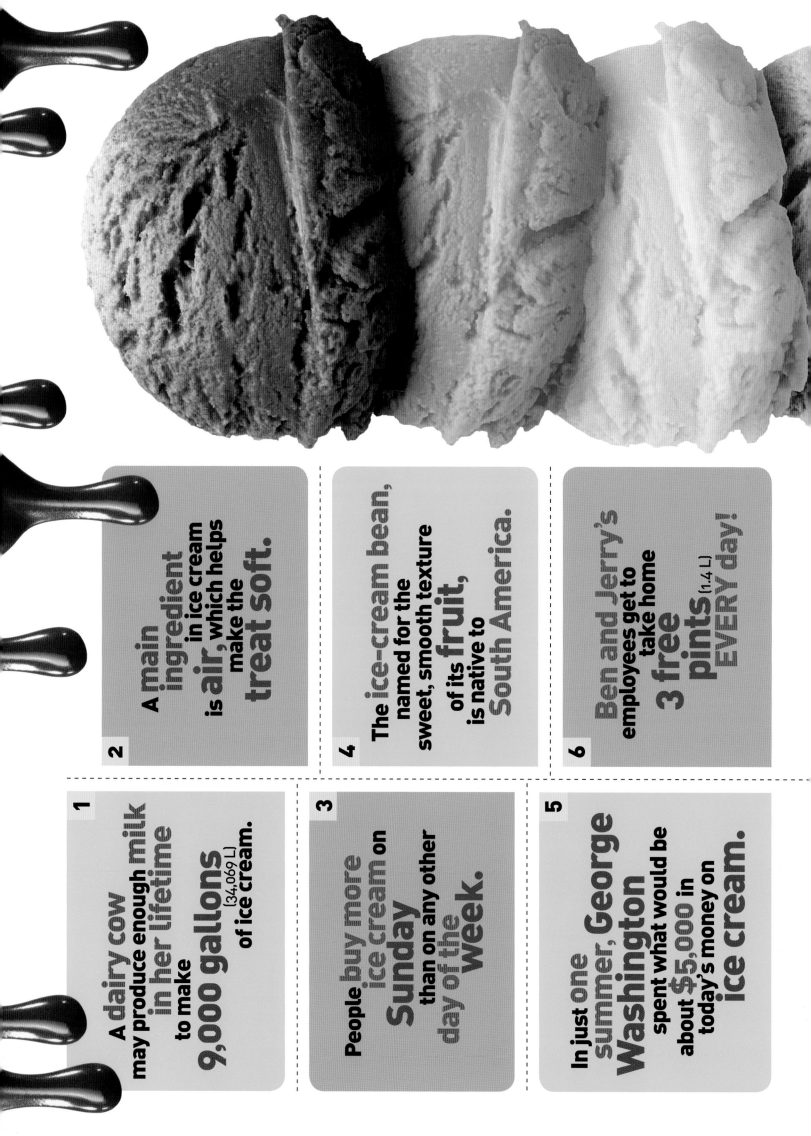

2

A main
ingredient
in ice cream
is air, which helps
make the
treat soft.

4

The ice-cream bean,
named for the
sweet, smooth texture
of its fruit,
is native to
South America.

6

Ben and Jerry's
employees get to
take home
3 free
pints (1.4 L)
EVERY day!

1

A dairy cow
may produce enough milk
in her lifetime
to make
9,000 gallons (34,069 L)
of ice cream.

3

People buy more
ice cream on
Sunday
than on any other
day of the
week.

5

In just one
summer, George
Washington
spent what would be
about $5,000 in
today's money on
ice cream.

Mouthwatering
Facts About
Ice Cream

7

A man once balanced **121 ice-cream scoops** on **one cone.**

8

You can get **pizza-flavored ice cream** in Philadelphia, PA, U.S.A.

9

Rock salt is used to make ice cream because ice and salt together reach a **colder temperature** than ice alone.

10

It takes about **50 licks** to finish a **scoop of ice cream.**

1
According to
Viking lore,
the god Odin rode an
eight-legged horse.

2
The spirits of
old umbrellas
appear in some
Japanese myths.

3
To **live forever,**
gods in ancient Chinese myths
ate peaches
from a magic tree.

4
One **cyclops**
from Greek mythology
liked to **snack**
on humans.

5
An Irish folklore hero
carried a spear made of
sea monster bones.

6
Every October,
people along the
Mekong River
in Thailand claim to see the
Naga fireballs
rising from the water—
legends say they come
from a fire-spitting
snake.

7
Baron Samedi is a
voodoo god usually shown
as a skeleton
wearing a top hat,
coattails, and sunglasses.

8

In Hawaii, U.S.A., there's a legend about **Nanaue,** who is **half-man** and **half-shark.**

9

More than half the population of **Iceland** believes in *huldufólk,* a hidden community of **elves, dwarves, and ghosts.**

10

Certain African tales feature a snake that **belches out rainbows.**

Epic Facts
About
Mythology

Cyclops vs. Odysseus from Greek mythology

11

1

T. rex could gulp **100 pounds** (45.4 kg) of meat at once.

2

Some **giant dinosaurs** had brains the size of Ping-Pong balls.

3

Mamenchisaurus's neck stretched up to **35 feet** (10.7 m).

4

Dinosaurs **survived** more than 800 times longer than humans have lived **on Earth.**

5

Some **dinosaurs** were no bigger than **chickens.**

6

Microraptor had **feathered wings** but likely couldn't fly.

7

Velociraptor could run about **25 miles** an hour (40.2 km/h).

Acrotholus audeti

8
The **longest** dinosaur name,
Micropachycephalosaurus,
belongs to one of the
smallest dinosaurs.

9
The biggest
dinosaur eggs could
hold about as much fluid as
**85 large
chicken eggs.**

10
Scientists
once thought
Stegosaurus
had a
second brain
**in its
rear end.**

Bite-Size
Facts About
Dinosaurs

What's the Difference?

Check out these similar pairings and see how you can determine this from that!

SQUID VS. OCTOPUS

They're both slippery, slimy, blue-blooded sea creatures that live in salt water, but squids and octopuses have some major differences! Everyone knows that an octopus has eight legs, but a squid actually has 10—eight plus two extra special tentacles that help them reach out and grab food. An octopus is very flexible (and can fit into extremely small spaces) because it doesn't have any shell; a squid has an internal shell that works like a backbone. And just because they both show up on dinner plates around the world doesn't mean they're all small and easy to catch—some octopuses grow to about 16 feet (5 m), and giant squid can reach 25 feet (7.6 m). It's a good thing both creatures tend to live alone, since their size isn't the only intimidating factor: Some octopuses are poisonous, and the giant squid is so fierce, it can battle a sperm whale and live to tell the tale!

YAM VS. SWEET POTATO

You may like yours topped with toasty marshmallows or mashed with butter and brown sugar. But what's the real difference between these starchy roots? You may think you know, but the truth will surprise you—chances are, you've probably never even eaten a true yam! Sweet potatoes come in a variety of colors—from white to orange to purple—and can be either firm or very soft when cooked. Yams, on the other hand, generally come from Africa or Asia and have a much harder skin. And despite their similar appearance, yams aren't in the potato family at all! So where does all that confusion come from? Stores sometimes label those deep orange sweet potatoes as "yams" to show the difference among the paler varieties. Those candied yams that Grandma makes for Thanksgiving? Not yams at all!

CAPITOL VS. CAPITAL

English is a language filled with many pesky homonyms (words that are spelled or pronounced the same, but have different meanings). One of the most commonly confused sets of words is capitol and capital, which are a special kind of homonym called a homophone (words that sound the same but are spelled differently and mean different things). You use capital when referring to capital letters, state capitals, a particularly nasty crime, something that is really excellent, and certain types of money. You use capitol only when talking about the building that Congress or a state government meets in. A nifty way to remember: Capitol with an "o" only has "o"ne definition. The only catch: Two major U.S. cities have neighborhoods called Capitol Hill: Seattle, in Washington State, and, of course, Washington, D.C.

ASTROLOGY VS. ASTRONOMY

Twinkle, twinkle, little star, how I wonder what the differences between astronomy and astrology are? The people peeping through those mega telescopes are astronomers, whose job it is to look at the what, where, why, and how of planets, stars, and other objects in space. They use math, science, and computing to explain how the universe works. Astrologers, on the other hand, are more interested in how the positions of the cosmos affect things here on Earth. For example, they believe where the sun and moon are on your birthdate can tell you what your future holds! Both astronomy and astrology are ancient practices, but scientists favor the real results of astronomy over the maybe-it's-true-and-maybe-it's-not theories of astrology.

EFFECT VS. AFFECT

Here's a little quiz: Do you know when to use "effect" and when to use "affect"? It's one of those little English mix-ups that confuse even the most experienced readers and writers! Part of the problem is that the words sound so similar, but what makes choosing the right one even more complicated is that they mean almost the same thing, too. In general, "affect" is used as a verb meaning "to make a change or difference to." "Effect" is usually a noun meaning "a result or consequence." For example: Adding chocolate chips affected the cookies' taste. Adding chocolate chips had the effect of a more delicious cookie. Still unclear? Remember that affect is usually an action, and let those "a's" remind you that they belong together.

reef squid

One type of squid will detach part of one of its own arms to distract an attacking predator.

A yam is more closely related to a lily than to a sweet potato.

The dome of the U.S. Capitol in Washington, D.C., was made with almost 9 million pounds (4,082 t) of iron.

Nostradamus, a 16th-century French astrologer, predicted many things, including when the world might end. But since his predictions go to the year 3797, we will have to wait.

15

Wacky Facts
About
Weather

1

Supercells— **giant thunderstorms** made of **swirling winds** that rise into the sky— can be **50,000 feet** (15,240 m) **tall.**

2

Hailstones can contain **pebbles, insects,** and even **nuts.**

3

A **moonbow** is a **rainbow caused by moonlight,** not sunlight, refracted by moisture in the air.

4

Some **raindrops** are shaped like **hamburger buns.**

5

Brontophobia is the fear of **thunder.**

6

Antarctica is the only continent where a **tornado** has never been recorded, though scientists say **it's possible** for one to occur there.

7

One weather-forecasting tool tests **strands of human hair** to check **humidity.**

8

Frogs are said to **croak louder** when bad weather is approaching.

9

The **Greeks** and **Romans** coined the phrase **"dog days of summer"** for the position of **Sirius, the dog star,** in the sky during midsummer.

10

Waterspouts, which are like **tornadoes** that happen over bodies of water, can **suck up fish, frogs, and turtles,** and cause them to **rain from the sky.**

tornado in Kansas, U.S.A.

Incredibly Odd Laws
in the U.S.A.

1 In **San Francisco,** California, the law forbids **spitting on laundry.**

2 In Connecticut, a **pickle** has to **bounce** in order to be called a pickle.

3 Owning **confetti** is **not allowed** in Mobile, Alabama.

4 You can legally take **roadkill** home and **cook it for dinner** in Montana.

5 It's against the law to **hoot** loudly after **11 p.m.** on weekdays in Athens, Georgia.

6 It was once a crime to **look gloomy** in Pocatello, Idaho.

7 People in Florida are banned from **keeping pigs** in **Miami Beach.**

8 Since 1973, it's been illegal to **collect seaweed at night** in New Hampshire.

9 **Riding a horse** faster than **10 miles an hour** (16.1 km/h) in the streets of Indianapolis, Indiana, **is prohibited.**

10 SASQUATCH XING

By law, **you cannot** purposely **harm Bigfoot** in Skamania County, Washington.

Bold Facts to

Color

Your World

1

It can take about
20 seconds
for a chameleon
to change color.

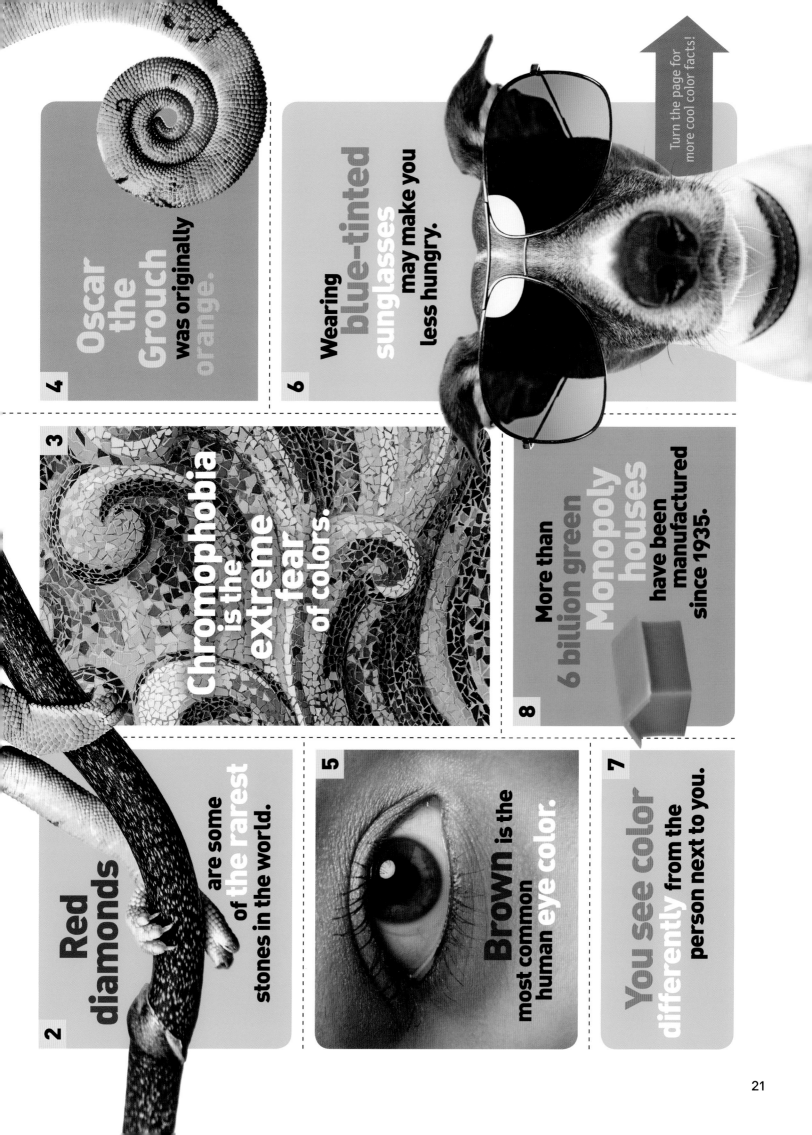

Turn the page for more cool color facts!

4

Oscar the Grouch was originally orange.

6

Wearing **blue-tinted sunglasses** may make you less hungry.

3

Chromophobia is the extreme **fear** of colors.

8

More than **6 billion green Monopoly houses** have been manufactured since 1935.

2

Red diamonds are some of the rarest stones in the world.

5

Brown is the most common human eye color.

7

You see color differently from the person next to you.

11 Darker-colored frozen pops usually **melt faster** than lighter ones.

14 More men **are color-blind** than women.

15 A **red flag** was a signal for battle in ancient Rome.

17 The fruit **orange got its name before** the color orange.

10 Red and yellow make you feel **hungry and happy,** which is why **fast-food chains** use these colors most.

13 There is a crayon color called **"macaroni and cheese."**

9 In Senegal, there's a lake that appears **bright pink,** thanks to a type of bacteria that lives in the water.

12 In parts of England, having a **black sheep** in a flock was considered lucky.

16 In ancient China, **only emperors** could wear yellow.

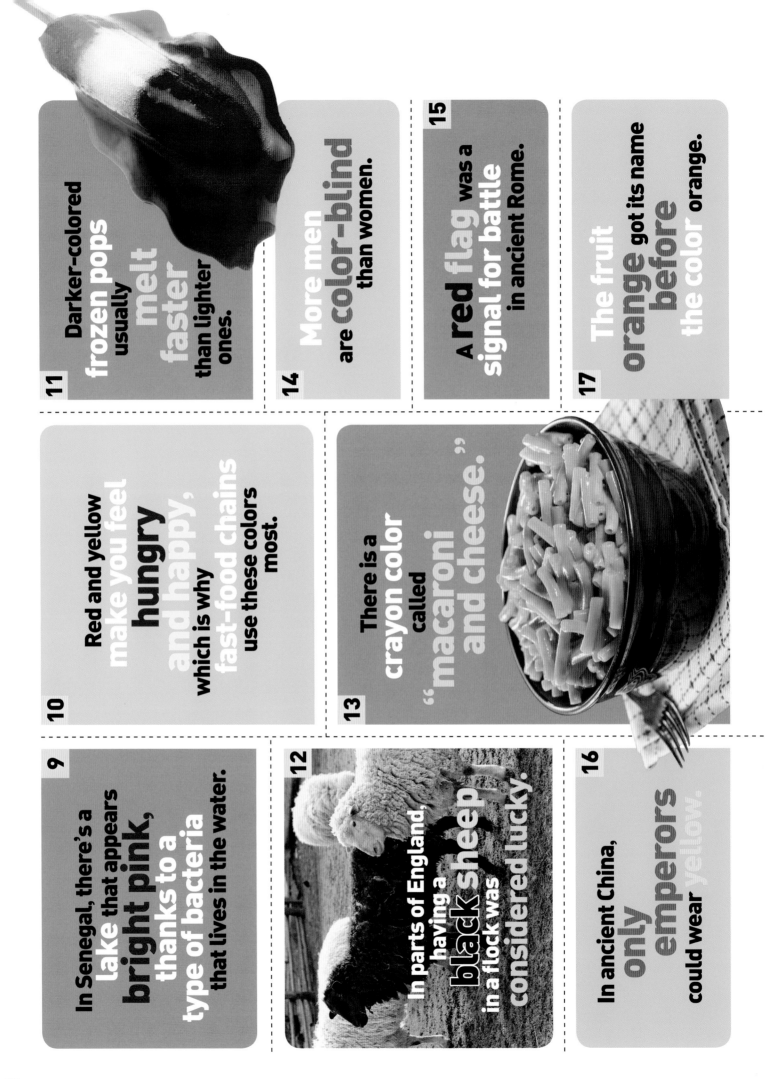

22

20

Studies show that painting your room **blue** could make you more creative.

19

Butterflies can **see more colors** than humans can.

18

The word "**purple**" comes from a Greek word for a type of shellfish.

1

Baby tapirs are born with white stripes and spots that disappear by the time they reach adulthood.

2

Born on land, poison dart frog tadpoles wriggle onto a parent's back for a ride to water.

3

Meerkat family members may curl up together to stay warm.

Fantastic
Facts About
Families

4

Mother **elephants** use their trunks to **lift newborns** to their feet.

5

European **shrew families** often travel with **each member** holding on to another's **tail.**

6

Some **male penguins** use smooth pebbles to "**propose**" to females.

7

African elephants are pregnant for longer than any land animal— more than twice the length of human pregnancies.

8

Cassowaries— large, flightless birds— are raised by **their dads.**

9

Baby Nile **crocodile** siblings "**chirp**" in **chorus** to **warn their family** of danger.

10

Up to **700 black widow** spiders can hatch from one grape-size egg.

meerkats

1 Ancient people may have mistaken **dinosaur bones** for **dragon remains.**

2 The **flag of Wales** features a **red dragon.**

3 Some stories claim that **dragon eggs** took **3,000 years to hatch.**

4 **Dragons** in very old **South American tales** had **feathers.**

5 The **capital of Vietnam** was once known as Thang Long or **"Soaring Dragon."**

6 **Draco**, the Latin word for **"dragon,"** is the name of a dragon-shaped **constellation.**

7 **People in China** once thought dragons **controlled rain.**

8 Long ago in Europe, people believed **dragon's blood cured illness.**

9 In parts of Asia, these **mythical creatures** were considered **kind.**

dragon sculpture in Xi'an, China

In an old English tale, **St. George** defeated a dragon by hiding under a **magical orange tree.**

Fiery
Facts About
Dragons

Facts That Are Too Hot to Handle

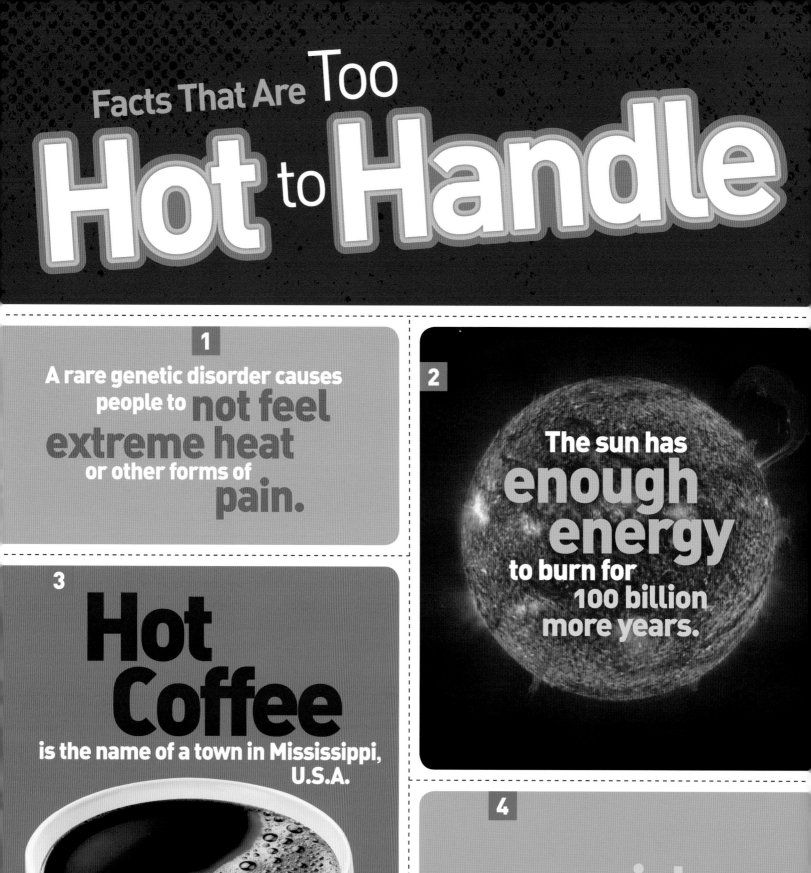

1
A rare genetic disorder causes people to **not feel extreme heat** or other forms of **pain.**

2
The sun has **enough energy** to burn for 100 billion more years.

3
Hot Coffee is the name of a town in Mississippi, U.S.A.

4
Cold water **weighs just a little bit more** than hot water.

5

A camel doesn't sweat until its body temperature reaches 106°F (41°C).

6

Pigs can get sunburned.

7

A baseball will travel farther in hot weather than in cold weather.

8

The hottest stars are blue.

9

Lightning hits the United States at least 22 million times a year.

10

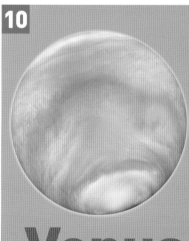

Venus is the hottest planet in our solar system.

Brachiosaurus

would be

tall
enough

to look through a

fifth-floor
window.

1 Mars, which is covered in **red rust,** is nicknamed **the red planet.**

2 A year on Mars lasts nearly **twice as long** as one **on Earth.**

3 One **volcano** on the planet is about **3 times taller** than **Mount Everest.**

Curiosity rover

4 It takes **6 to 11 months** for a spacecraft to **travel** from Earth to Mars.

8 **The sky** on Mars appears to be the color of **butterscotch.**

5 **Mars** has 2 small **moons.**

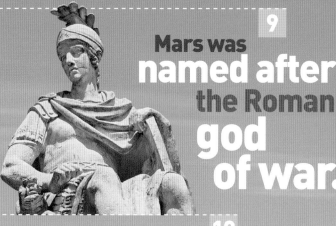

9 Mars was **named after** the Roman **god** **of war.**

6 By 2035, astronauts **may visit** Mars.

7 You could **jump** 3 times higher on Mars than you can on Earth.

10 The average **temperature** on Mars is **-81°F** (-63°C).

Megacool Facts
About
Mars

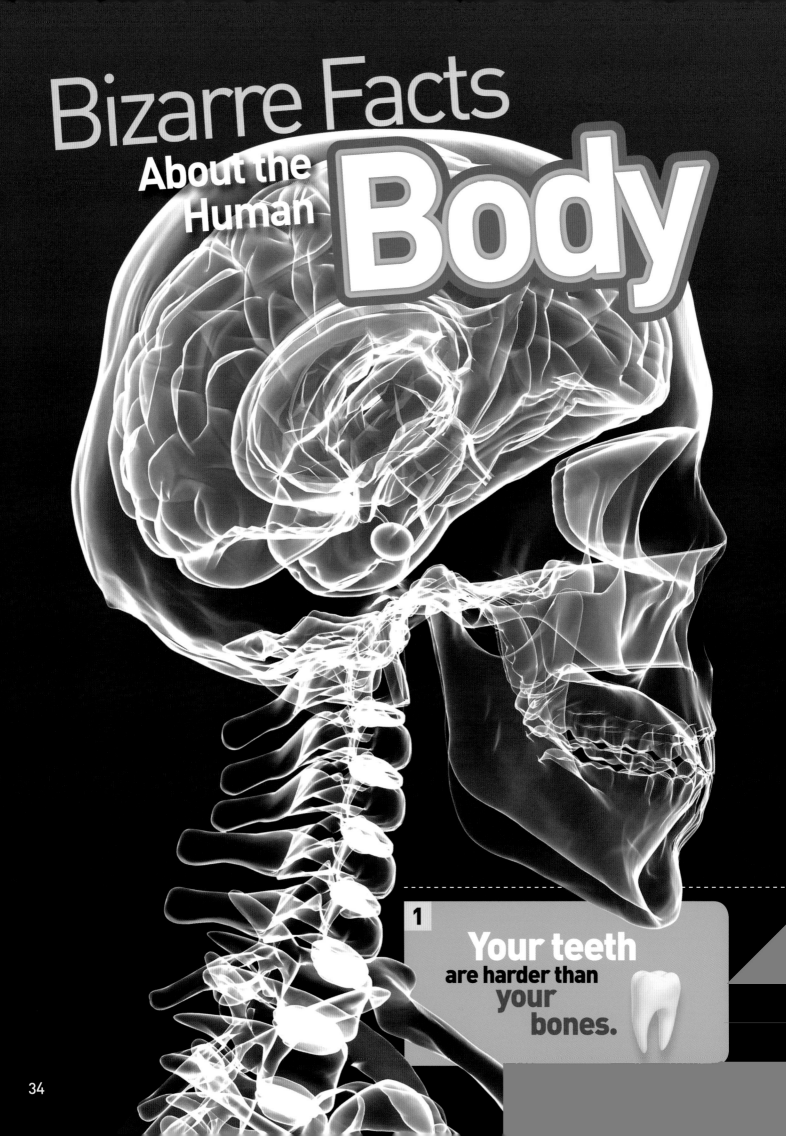

Bizarre Facts

About the Human

Body

1

Your teeth
are harder than
your
bones.

2 Brain cells live longer than all the other cells in your body.

3 People's tongue prints are as unique as their fingerprints.

4 The saliva you produce in your lifetime could fill nearly 30,000 water bottles.

5 There are thousands of different bacteria that can live inside belly buttons—the average person has somewhere around 65.

6 Your heart beats about 100,000 times each day.

7 You can buy fake eyebrows and eyelashes made of real hair.

8 Your hair grows faster in warm weather.

9 You can't move your body when you dream.

10 Some people can hear their eyeballs moving.

Turn the page for more odd body facts!

11
The more you **concentrate,** the less **you blink.**

12
If you eat too many **carrots,** your skin can **turn orange.**

13
Fingernails grow faster than toenails.

14
According to one study, **six-year-olds laugh** about **300 times** per day— adults **less than 100.**

15
About one-quarter of the body's **bones** are **in the feet—** that's **52** out of more than **200!**

16
The human **brain** may be able to read **1,000 words per minute,** but most people average about 200.

17
Your eyes can see about 10 million **different colors.**

18
The length of **your foot** is about the same as the distance from your **elbow to your wrist.**

19
The average human heart **beats** about **three billion** times in a lifetime.

20
Humans and
great apes
have about the
same number of
hairs.

Money Facts You Can Bank On

1

Most U.S. dollar bills **circulate** for about **5-6 years.**

2

The cost of **making a penny** is almost double its value, so **millions of dollars** are lost **each year** to produce them.

IN GOD WE TRUST

LIBERTY

2006

3

The average 10-year-old earns about $8.50 a week from allowance and small jobs.

4

A dollar bill **can be folded** in the same spot about **4,000 times** before it **tears.**

5 As of 2013, the clock on the new hundred-dollar bill says 10:30.

6 A standard Monopoly game contains $15,140 in fake money.

7 In 2007, Canada released the world's *first* one-million-dollar coin, which weighed **220** pounds. (100 kg)

8 A line of **84,702 pennies** would stretch for a mile. (1.6 km)

9 The most expensive item ever sold on an online auction site was a **$168 million** yacht.

10 Salt was once used as currency.

1 Food passes through the **giant squid's** brain on the way to its stomach.

2 Cockroaches have lived on Earth for some **365 million years**—more than 2,000 times longer than humans.

3 Some sea stars break off their own **arms** when frightened.

4 The barking pigeon has a call that sounds like a **loud dog.**

5 A **sea turtle** can weigh as much as a **water buffalo.**

6 An alligator grows about **3,000 teeth** in a lifetime.

7 A newborn kangaroo is about as long as a **paper clip.**

8 Warthogs don't have **warts.**

9 Every zebra's **stripe pattern** is unique— like your **fingerprints.**

10 Elephants sometimes make a **purr-like sound** when content.

Wild
Facts About
Animals

"ICE" Castle

Only about **5 percent** of Turkey is in Europe; the rest is in Asia.

Until 1934, most Turkish people **didn't** have last names.

Why this frozen-looking landscape is a hot spot!

Seemingly snowy cliffs loom over a valley in Denizli Province, Turkey (a country that straddles Europe and Asia). Embedded in the frozen-looking bluffs are tiers of small, turquoise blue pools—it's almost as if parts of the formation are melting. Despite its appearance, the site is far from frigid. In fact, water here can sometimes reach triple digits. And those aren't icy cliffs—they're limestone rock formations. Known as Pamukkale (PAH-moo-KAH-leh) in the Turkish language, or Cotton Castle in English, the oddness of this area has made it a popular place to chill.

IN HOT WATER

Cotton Castle towers about 325 feet (99 m) in the air and stretches nearly 9,000 feet (2,743 m) long. The landform has 17 hot springs at the top. Hot springs are geothermal wells that spout up from inside the Earth. Warmed by magma (or hot, liquid rock) before it surfaces, the spring water here is a toasty 95°F (35°C) to 140°F (60°C).

The formation's hot springs are the result of activity below Earth's surface. As tectonic plates that are in the planet's crust shift, they cause earthquakes. This forces the water above ground. The springs are the reason for Cotton Castle's odd, icy appearance.

OH, THAT'S RICH!

The water in the springs is full of minerals, naturally occurring chemicals, and calcium carbonate (which is like chalk). The mineral-rich H_2O comes to the surface and trickles down the walls. When the calcium carbonate in the water meets carbon dioxide in the air, it can form a jellylike substance that piles up as it makes its way down the cliff. Eventually the jelly dries and hardens into terraces of white limestone rock called travertine. This is what gives the cliffs their frozen appearance.

Some of the water also accumulates in the shallow basins that dot the edge of the formation, creating pools. Because the water cools several degrees as it flows into the pools, it's possible to dip your toes in some of these natural hot tubs.

The process that created this wacky landform has gone on for tens of thousands of years. And people have been trekking to Cotton Castle since ancient times to peek at the odd spot.

RELAXATION STATION

Cotton Castle has been a popular attraction since around 200 B.C., when a king founded a town called Hierapolis near the site. People believed that the hot springs had healing powers. By the 1970s, Cotton Castle was so popular that hotels were constructed nearby. Some were even built on top of it.

Unfortunately the construction caused sections of Cotton Castle to crumble, and heavy foot traffic turned some pools brown. Fearing the pristine landform would disappear for good, officials declared it a protected World Heritage site to prevent any future damage from happening to the area. The hotels were soon torn down, and now only some pools are open to visitors. With these safeguards in place, Cotton Castle will hopefully be around for many years to come, its icelike beauty frozen in time.

Tulips **originated** in this country.

The Turkish alphabet has **29 letters.**

The capital of the Roman Empire was **moved from Rome** in what is now Italy to Turkey.

Fetching Facts About Canines

1 A dog's **nose print** is as **unique as a** human **fingerprint.**

2 The **basenji,** a dog from Africa, **yodels** instead of **barks.**

3 **Dalmatian** puppies are born **without spots.**

4 A miniature **schnauzer-poodle** mix is called a **schnoodle.**

5 Chocolate, avocado, grapes, and **onions** are just a few of the **human foods** that can make dogs **very sick.**

6 The **Chihuahua** is the world's **smallest** dog breed.

7

Some dogs can reportedly detect **cancer,** low **blood sugar, anxiety,** and **seizures** in humans.

8

You can buy a **diamond dog collar** for about **3 million dollars.**

9

George Washington had a **Dalmatian** named **Sweetlips.**

10

Tia the Neapolitan mastiff **gave birth** to **24 puppies** in **one litter.**

45

Page-Turning
Facts About
Books

1
Treasure Island was **inspired by a map** that author Robert Louis Stevenson drew with his 12-year-old stepson.

2
In an early version, Roald Dahl's *James and the Giant Peach* featured a **giant cherry.**

3
In L. Frank Baum's *The Wonderful Wizard of Oz,* **Dorothy's shoes** are described as **silver.**

4
In Japanese, the word ***tsundoku*** refers to buying books that you **don't actually read.**

5

Percy Jackson and the Olympians began as a **bedtime** story for author Rick Riordan's son.

6

Dr. Seuss wrote **Green Eggs and Ham** on a bet from his editor, who said he couldn't write a book using **just 50 words.**

7

Each book in R. L. Stine's **Goosebumps** series took about **8 days to write.**

8

J.K. Rowling considered calling the final **Harry Potter** book *Harry Potter and the Elder Wand.*

9

A **5-by-7-foot** (1.5-by-2.1-cm) book full of **pictures of Bhutan** is the **largest book** in the Library of Congress.

10

Where the Wild Things Are was originally supposed to be about horses, but author and illustrator Maurice Sendak **couldn't draw horses—** instead, the "wild things" were inspired by **his relatives.**

Food Facts to Drool Over

1 Fairy floss is another name for cotton candy.

2 A 20-ounce (591-ml) bottle of soda has more than twice as much sugar as some candy bars.

3
One acre (0.4 ha) of peanut plants can produce 30,000 peanut butter-and-jelly sandwiches.

4
One cherry pie baked in British Columbia, Canada, weighed nearly 40,000 pounds (18,144 kg).

5
Strawberries contain more vitamin C than oranges.

6
The ingredient that causes most types of peanut butter to be spreadable comes from seaweed.

7
Fried tarantulas are considered a delicacy in Cambodia.

8
There is a variety of lemon called baboon.

9
Rock candy was once used as medicine.

10
Fortune cookies originated in Japan, not China.

Turn the page for more fabulous food facts!

11 **Nachos** were invented in 1943 by a **Mexican man named Ignacio,** nicknamed "Nacho," who worked at a restaurant in the Mexican town of **Piedras Negras.**

12 The **first Thanksgiving** dinner may have included **eels.**

13 A couple exchanged **wedding vows** inside a 7,000-pound [3,175-kg] **bowl of pasta.**

14 You can **wrestle someone** in a pit of **mashed potatoes** at a Minnesota, U.S.A., festival.

15 A restaurant in Taiwan **serves meals** in bowls shaped like **toilets.**

16 Most **farmed carrots** used to be **purple.**

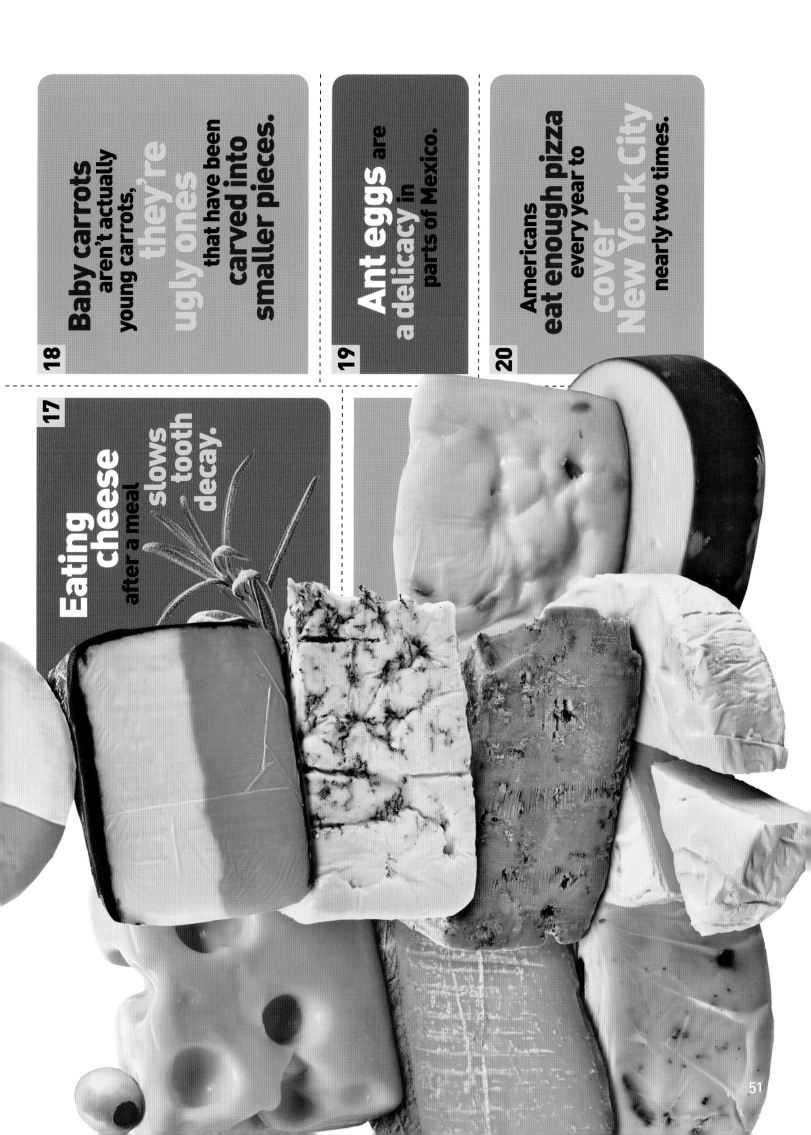

18

Baby carrots aren't actually young carrots, **they're ugly ones** that have been **carved into smaller pieces.**

19

Ant eggs are a delicacy in parts of Mexico.

20

Americans eat enough pizza every year to **cover New York City** nearly two times.

17

Eating cheese after a meal **slows tooth decay.**

Frosty Snow

Facts About

1 "**Snirt**" is slang for **snow** combined with **dirt.**

2 The **tallest snowman** ever built was higher than a **10-story** building.

3 The world's largest **snowball fight** involved **7,681** participants in Saskatchewan, Canada, in January 2016.

4 **Twenty inches** (50.8 cm) of snow equals **one inch** of water (2.54 cm) on average.

5 Snowflakes **get smaller** as the temperature **drops.**

6

Some **avalanches** can travel more than **100 miles an hour** (161 km/h).

7

The word **Himalaya** means "**house of snow.**"

8

Snow is actually **translucent,** not white.

9

Chionophobia is the **extreme fear** of snow.

10

Almost **90 percent** of snow is **air.**

PANDA INVASION

WHAT Animal sculptures

WHERE Berlin, Germany

DETAILS This is what a panda party looks like. A conservation group placed miniature giant panda sculptures in front of a train station in the German capital to raise awareness of the endangered species. The 1,600 animals represent how many of the real-life versions are still left in the wild. It would take a lot of bamboo to feed these little guys.

Extreme Weirdness

SKIING TOILET

WHAT Outhouse race

WHERE Anchorage, Alaska, U.S.A.

DETAILS This event brings new meaning to "potty training." Alaska's most populous city hosts a winter festival each year to celebrate the state's history. A crowd favorite is the outhouse race, in which residents paint outhouses, or outdoor bathrooms, before pushing them through town on skis. Wonder if the prize is a golden plunger?

WATERFALL OF BOOKS

WHAT Book tower

WHERE Madrid, Spain

DETAILS If you've ever felt like throwing your school-books out the window, this might be for you. Supported by a metal frame, the tower of books holds 5,000 pieces of lit-erature so they appear to pour out of a second-story window. You can't do that with e-books.

GIANTS HIT THE BEACH

WHAT Seaside sculptures

WHERE Sydney, Australia

DETAILS Talk about tough guys—this pair is literally made of steel. The eight-foot (2.4-m)-high pieces, titled "Heads Up," were part of a free outdoor exhibit across 1.2 miles (1.9 km) of Australian beaches. Over a hun-dred sculptures by artists from around the globe were featured.

SPACE RACE

WHAT Spacecraft-shaped race car

WHERE Kiev, Ukraine

DETAILS We doubt this vehicle is NASA-approved. Inspired by a lunar rover, the cart was part of a race against about 50 other wacky-looking transports, including one vehicle that looked like a cucumber and another with a colorful *Alice in Wonderland* theme. That's quite a road show.

GIRAFFES GO SHOPPING

WHAT Stilt walkers

WHERE Tokyo, Japan

DETAILS Bet you can spot some tall deals at this mall. A French theater group dressed up in stilts—some wearing giraffe necks to make themselves 26 feet (7.9 m) tall—to celebrate the 10th anniversary of a local entertainment complex. Performers wore red to symbolize love, the event's theme, and were joined by a clown.

TIGER RUNS MARATHONS

WHAT Tiger costume

WHERE Agra, India

DETAILS Finishing a marathon (a 26.2-mile [42.2-km] race) is definitely impressive—but not as impressive as completing one with a big cat on your back. Wildlife photographer Paul Goldstein has run in 13 marathons while wearing this 30-pound (13.6-kg) tiger costume. His attention-grabbing outfit has raised thousands of dollars for tiger charities around the world.

1 The **first** nonstop **balloon flight** around the **world** took 19 days, 21 hours, and 55 minutes.

2 Daredevil David "The Bullet" Smith has been **shot out of a cannon** more than **5,000 times.**

3 A special airline allows only pets as passengers.

4 The fastest **baseball pitches** reach speeds of more than a **100 miles an hour.** (161 km/h)

5 **640** is the record for the **most parachute jumps** in 24 hours.

6 **Bullfrogs** have traveled into **space.**

Uplifting Facts About Flight

7

A **flying lizard** can glide as far as **100 feet—** (30.5 m) about the length of 17 lined-up **bicycles.**

8

A song sparrow's heart beats more than **540 times** a minute.

9

The speediest **manned aircraft** flew across the United States in one hour and four minutes— **four hours faster** than a passenger jet!

10

One of the world's **biggest kites** is almost as wide as a **football field.**

Luck

Fortunate Facts About

2 **Breaking glass** is considered to bring good luck in Bulgaria.

3 **Pigs** are signs of **prosperity** and **good luck** in China.

5 Seeing a **white horse** facing you is said to bring you luck in Wales, in the United Kingdom.

1 People in Spain eat **12 grapes** on **New Year's Eve** for luck.

4 Watching a **ladybug** fly into your bedroom is considered good luck in Italy.

6 In Germany, it's good luck to touch a **chimney sweep's brush.**

7 Only **1 in 10,000** clovers has **four leaves.**

9 Many people believe crossing **their fingers** brings **good luck.**

8 Riding a **camel** could bring you luck in Turkey.

10 It's considered good luck to carry **bat bones** in your pocket in Greece.

Turn the page for more lucky facts!

12

Some people believe

lucky horseshoes

should be hung **facing up;** others think they're luckier **facing down.**

13

A 2011 poll ranked "lucky" as the **16th most popular dog name.**

15

Several cultures believe that getting **pooped on by a bird** brings good fortune.

11

In New Orleans, LA, U.S.A., during Mardi Gras, colorful **king cakes** are baked with a **tiny plastic baby** inside—the person who gets the baby **in their slice** is supposed to receive good luck.

14

Triskaidekaphobia is the fear of the **number 13.**

16

Wearing **yellow underwear** on New Year's Day in Peru is considered lucky.

17

Tuesday—not Friday—the 13th is an **unlucky date** in Latin America, Spain, and Greece.

18

Holding a **rabbit's foot** is said to bring luck in parts of West Africa.

19

In China, it's considered lucky to have **moles** on your face.

20

In England, a bride finding a **spider** in her **wedding dress** is considered lucky.

Vibrant Facts
About the Color Red

1

The **Red Sea** is the **warmest sea** in the world.

2

The word **"ruby"** comes from the Latin word **rubens,** which means "red."

3

also means **"beautiful"** in Russia.

4

The red **stripes** on the United States flag stand for **courage.**

There are **at least 23** different shades of **red crayons.**

5

6 The smallest **red peppers** are usually the **hottest.**

7 The color red **doesn't** really make bulls **angry;** they are **color-blind.**

8 As few as **2 percent** of people in the **United States** have **red hair.**

9 The **scarlet ibis** gets its color from the crabs it eats.

STOP

10 The first **stop signs** were **black-and-white.**

Wonderful
Facts About
the World

1

The **Great Wall** of China spans roughly **4,500 miles**—[7,242 km] that's almost as long as the continent of **Africa.**

2

The **Nile River** is **longer** than the distance from Washington, D.C., to Los Angeles, California, U.S.A.

3

Oregon, U.S.A.'s **D River** is only **120 feet long**— shorter than an Olympic-size swimming pool. (36.6 m)

4

The **50 tallest** mountains in the world are **all in Asia.**

5

You have to climb a **293-step spiral staircase** to reach the top of the **Leaning Tower** of Pisa.

6

The surface of the **Atlantic Ocean** is **saltier** than the surface of the Pacific Ocean.

7

The **lowest temperature** on Earth (-136°F) [-57.8°C] was recorded in **Antarctica.**

8

Death Valley, California, is the **hottest place** in North America.

9

Australia's **Great Barrier Reef** can be seen **from space.**

10

About **one-tenth** of the Earth's surface is **covered with ice.**

Sweet Facts
About
Chocolate

1

A **record-setting** box of chocolates had **90,090** individual chocolates.

2

The average American **eats** more than **12 pounds** (5.4 kg) of chocolate a year. That's as heavy as some bowling balls!

3

The woman who **invented** chocolate chip cookies **sold the recipe** to Nestlé in exchange **for a lifetime supply** of chocolate.

4

Legend says that Aztec ruler **Moctezuma** drank 50 cups of chocolate a day.

5

There are about **1,000** chocolate chips in a **pound** of chocolate. (453 g)

6

Hershey's Kisses were probably named for the **puckering sound** made by the machine that first **produced** the candy.

7

The FDA allows up to **8 insect parts** in the average **chocolate bar.**

8

Blonde chocolate was reportedly discovered **by accident,** when a chef **overcooked** some white chocolate.

9

Maine, U.S.A., is home to a **1,700-pound** chocolate (771-kg) **moose** named Lenny.

10

A hundred-year-old chocolate bar sold for **nearly $700.**

ARCTIC VS. ANTARCTIC

You might confuse these two because of their strikingly similar names. But the truth is, they are two totally different places on opposite ends of the globe! Antarctica is the southernmost continent in the world. It's home to penguins and leopard seals ... and maybe a couple thousand people who moved there to work on the research bases set up in the coldest place in the world. The Arctic, on the other hand, is an icy ocean almost completely surrounded by land. It's warmer than Antarctica, making it more comfortable for both land and sea creatures—it's the only area in the world where you'll find polar bears. But even though it's warmer, the Arctic stays mighty cold: The average summer temperature is still freezing. Brrrrr!!!

What's the Difference?

CROCODILE VS. ALLIGATOR

In the big bad world of reptiles, there are two look-alikes that reign champion of the choppers—crocodiles and alligators. And while these beasts might appear to be twins, they are actually two totally different predators. Crocodiles are generally bigger and more aggressive than alligators, though there are a few varieties that break these rules. While wild alligators can only be found in the United States and China, crocodiles live all over the world. Want to know what you're facing? Take a look at the shape of its head. Alligators have a shorter, wider U-shaped snout, and crocodiles have a sharper V-shaped mouth that displays some of those pointy pearly whites. Alligators also commonly have a lighter skin color than crocodiles. Neither would be ideal pets!

RUGBY VS. AMERICAN FOOTBALL

This one is tricky, so let's start by getting one thing straight: American football is not what the rest of the world calls football. What the rest of the world calls football is called soccer in the U.S. and Canada—American football isn't even played outside of North America. As for the differences between American football and rugby? They may look similar, but they're actually very different games. Rugby is popular in parts of Europe, Australia, and Argentina—they wear far less protective gear than American football players. Even under the pads, NFL (National Football League) players suffer more injuries than rugby players because tackling is a bigger part of the game. Rugby gets more players on the field during a game—15 players, compared to football's 11. But those extra rugby players are covering a lot of ground, since the field is more than 50 percent bigger than American football fields! At least they don't have to run as long: Rugby games last less than two hours, not the three hours usual for the NFL. And finally, just so you know, rugby and soccer came first; football started in universities in the late 19th century.

PRESIDENT VS. MONARCH

In terms of jobs, there aren't many that are more difficult than running a whole country. But monarchs (otherwise known as kings and queens) come by this job differently. A president is chosen by the people and only fills the job for a specific time (in the U.S., four years, unless he or she is reelected). But a monarch is born into the role, which means some of them reign for their whole lives. In history, even babies have ended up as kings or queens—Mary Queen of Scots became queen of Scotland when she was just six days old! Presidents have some help with the job—in the U.S., they're supported by Congress and the Supreme Court. Monarchs generally have more cultural responsibilities than political ones—in England, the queen relies on Parliament to handle the government side of things. And what about a dictator? He or she makes the rules without any input!

DOLPHIN VS. PORPOISE

Unless you compare them side by side, dolphins and porpoises are easy to mix up. Both mammals—not fish!—use echolocation to "see" objects under water, and they communicate with the other members of their family by using high-frequency sounds like whistles. (Porpoises make a noise so high pitched that humans can't even hear it!) But dolphins live in large family groups called pods, and porpoises usually stay in smaller groups of two to four. There are a few physical differences, too: Dolphins have a sort of beaklike snout, and porpoises' are rounder; most dolphins are longer than porpoises and have a skinnier overall look; and porpoises have teeth that are flat and rectangular, where dolphins' are cone-shaped. Those squeaky creatures doing flips for a crowd? Those are almost always dolphins. Porpoises don't like being the star of the show!

NUT VS. LEGUME

Peanuts and hazelnuts and walnuts, oh my! Despite the fact that all three of these have "nut" in their name, they're actually from three different types of foods. Peanuts belong to the legume family (with black beans, green peas, and lentils) because they grow in a pod with more than one seed inside, and that pod starts to open when the plant is ready for harvest. Hazelnuts are called true nuts—they are single seeds inside the sort of very hard shell you need a nutcracker to break. Maybe the most interesting is that there's a third category of nuts called drupes. Drupes are actually a fleshy fruit with a seed inside; peaches, plums, and cherries are all examples, but so are walnuts and almonds—we just eat the seed instead of the fruit!

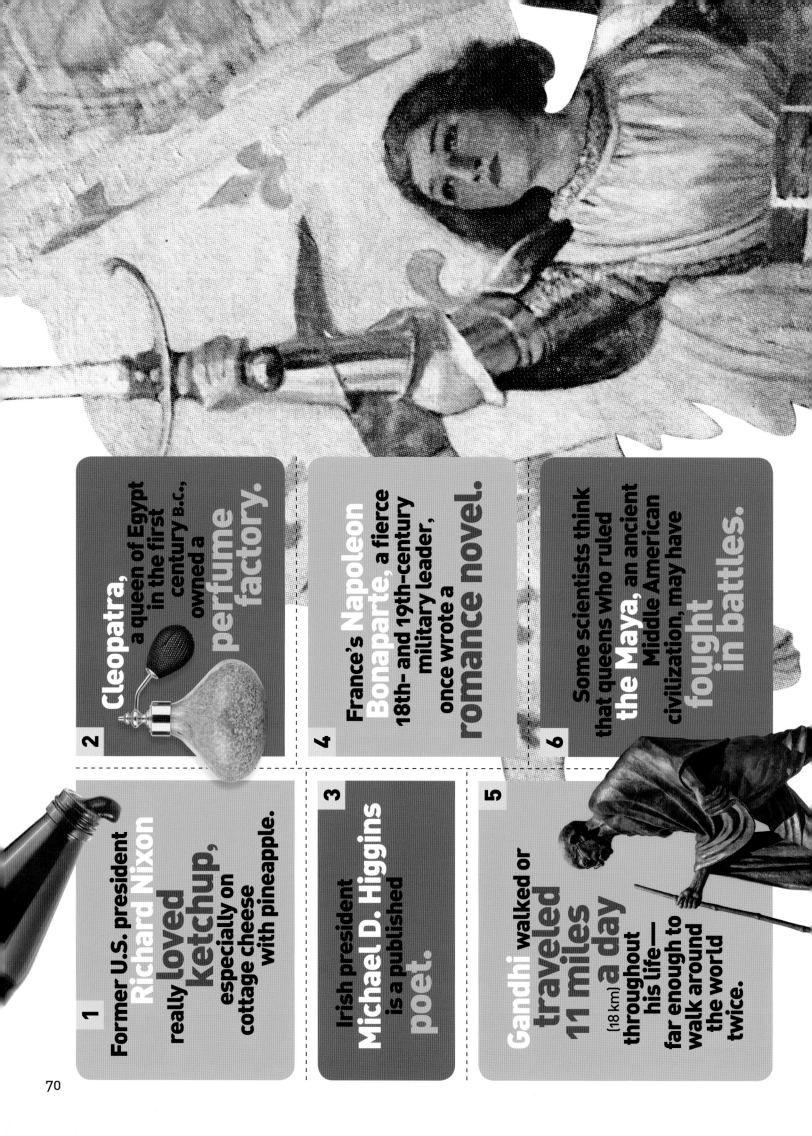

2

Cleopatra, a queen of Egypt in the first century B.C., owned a **perfume factory.**

4

France's Napoleon Bonaparte, a fierce 18th- and 19th-century military leader, once wrote a **romance novel.**

6

Some scientists think that queens who ruled the Maya, an ancient Middle American civilization, may have **fought in battles.**

1

Former U.S. president **Richard Nixon** really **loved ketchup,** especially on cottage cheese with pineapple.

3

Irish president **Michael D. Higgins** is a published **poet.**

5

Gandhi walked or **traveled 11 miles** (18 km) **a day** throughout his life— far enough to walk around the world twice.

Facts About Leaders Who Rule

Joan of Arc

7 **Queen Elizabeth II** of the United Kingdom can travel the world **without a passport.**

8 **King Kamehameha I,** who united the Hawaiian Islands in 1810, was known for his **surfing skills.**

9 Former U.S. president **Barack Obama** has read all 7 **Harry Potter** books.

10 **Joan of Arc** inspired the short "bob" hairstyle almost 500 years after she died.

Riveting
Facts About
Rain Forests

1

One-quarter of all **butterfly species** on Earth live in South American rain forests.

Morpho achilles

2

There are **more species** of fish in the Amazon River than in the Atlantic Ocean.

3

Antarctica is the only continent that has **no rain forests.**

4

Tropical rain forests are a **habitat** for **80 percent** of the world's **insect species.**

5

The Amazon rain forest is home to **giant rodents** called capybaras that are about **as tall as** German shepherds.

6

British Columbia, **Canada,** is home to a quarter of the world's temperate, or **cool weather**, rain forests.

7

The Western world only uses about 200 of the **3,000 different fruits** that grow in the rain forest.

8

The world's **biggest flower—** found in the Indonesian rain forest—can grow **wider than a car tire.**

9

In 2004, a hiker in Australia's Blue Mountains **discovered a tree** that everyone **thought had been extinct** for millions of years.

10

Rainbow-colored **grasshoppers** live in the rain forests of Peru.

Facts of Amazing Proportion

1

The **smallest** known **spider** is smaller than the period at the end of this sentence.

2

The **heaviest lizard,** the **Komodo dragon,** can weigh more than two grown women.

3

Vatican City in Italy is the world's smallest country, covering only **one-fifth of a square mile.** (0.5 sq km)

4

The **largest grilled cheese** sandwich ever made weighed more than a **baby elephant.**

5 The world's **longest beard** was more than **17 feet** (5.2 m) long and is stored in the Smithsonian.

6 More than **200 people** could fit inside the world's **biggest igloo.**

7 A beverage company created a **giant ice-cream float** made with **2,850 gallons** (10,788.4 L) **of cola and 7,200 scoops** of ice cream.

8 One of the world's **smallest museums** is a 22-foot (6.7-m) closet space dedicated to author **Edgar Allan Poe.**

9 Dubai's **Palm Islands,** a **man-made** archipelago actually **shaped like** a palm tree, is so big you can see it from **space.**

10 One of the **smallest dinosaurs,** a *Fruitadens,* was **about as tall as a toy poodle.**

75

Sweet Facts

About

Desserts

1 The largest s'more ever made used **40,000 marshmallows,** 8,000 chocolate bars, and 55,000 graham crackers.

2 The oldest **chocolate** ever found was in a **2,600-year-old** pot.

3 Thirty-five percent of Americans surveyed admitted to **eating pie** for breakfast.

4 You can buy a **cupcake-shaped** designer **handbag—** with strawberry- and chocolate- colored crystals— for **$4,295.**

5 **Olive oil** ice cream is a popular flavor in several **fancy restaurants.**

6 National **Parfait Day** is November 25.

7 Some **astronauts** living on the Mir space station **ate Jell-O** every Sunday to help keep track of the days.

8 A man once **ate 49** glazed doughnuts in **8 minutes.**

9 The word **"cookie"** comes from the Dutch word *koekje*, which means **"small cake."**

10 **Twinkies** originally had banana filling.

Incredible Facts About Your Impact on the World

In your lifetime, you will likely...

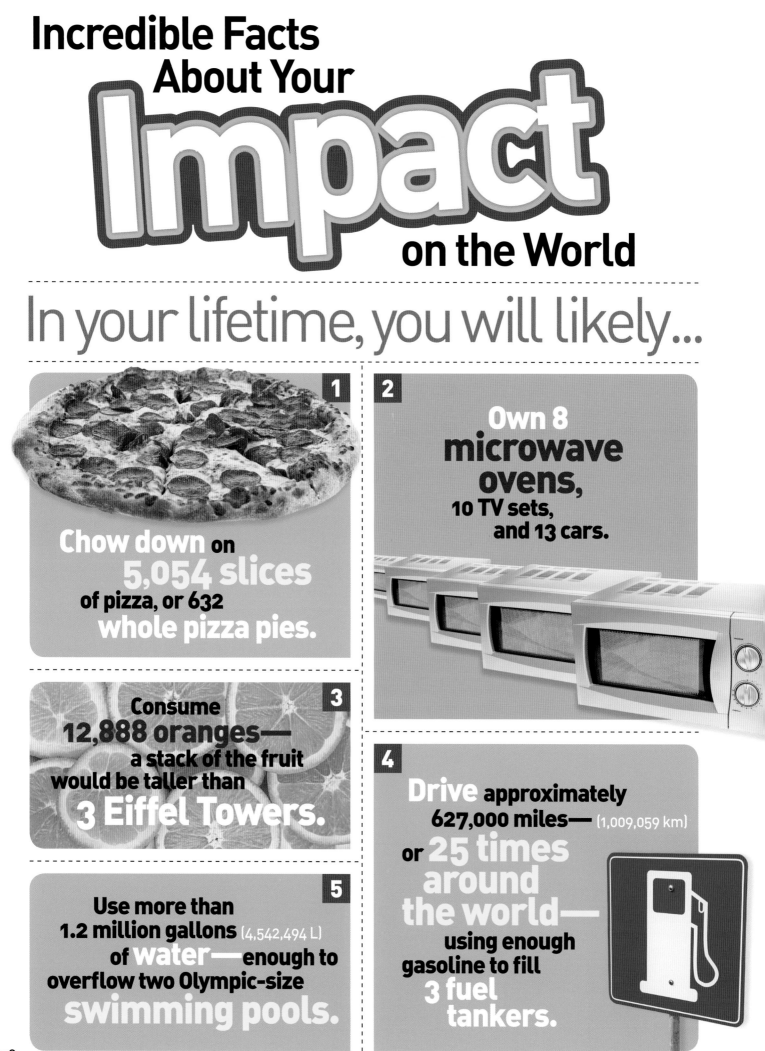

1 **Chow down** on **5,054 slices** of pizza, or 632 **whole pizza pies.**

2 Own 8 **microwave ovens,** 10 TV sets, and 13 cars.

3 Consume **12,888 oranges**—a stack of the fruit would be taller than **3 Eiffel Towers.**

4 **Drive** approximately 627,000 miles— (1,009,059 km) or **25 times around the world**— using enough gasoline to fill **3 fuel tankers.**

5 Use more than 1.2 million gallons (4,542,494 L) of **water**—enough to overflow two Olympic-size **swimming pools.**

6

Snack on 14,518 **candy bars,** which would fill up about 12 **shopping carts.**

7

Throw away enough **trash** to fill up about **five garbage trucks.**

8

Gobble down 9,917 pounds (4,498.3 kg) of **potatoes.** That's the weight of about eight average-size **racehorses.**

9

Scrub up with **656 bars of soap.** A tower of the soaps would stand taller than a **five-story building.**

10

Eat an amount of **hamburger** meat equal to the weight of a **family car.**

Fire trucks
were originally
painted
red

80

because that was the cheapest color.

1

When a **cheetah** accelerates, its **heart rate** may shoot from 120 to 250 beats a minute **in just seconds.**

2

The amount of **energy** created by your heart in a day could **power a car** for 20 miles. (32.2 km)

3

A zebrafish can **repair its heart** if the organ gets **damaged.**

4

Octopuses have **three** hearts.

5

There's a **heart-shaped coral reef** in Australia.

6

A woman's heart usually **beats faster** than a man's heart.

7

A huge **mangrove swamp** on the South Pacific island of New Caledonia is **naturally heart-shaped.**

8

An astronaut's heartbeat **slows down** in **outer space.**

9

Ancient Egyptians believed that **a person's soul** was located **in the heart.**

10

About **eight billion** conversation **heart candies** are produced every year— enough to wrap **around the moon** more than nine times.

Heart

Facts to Get You

Pumped

Mummy

Facts to Unwrap

2 In the 1800s, people attended shows **to watch performers unwrap mummies.**

1 It took about **8 hours** to bandage **the lead actor** in the 1932 movie *The Mummy.*

3 Mummies have been found on **every continent,** including **Antarctica.**

4 A mummy was once found with its **tongue sticking out.**

5 A 2,400-year-old mummy from Siberia had **fur balls** in her **eye sockets.**

6 A mummy in Italy from 1920 is so **well preserved** she looks as if she's **sleeping.**

7 One ancient mummy was **issued a passport** to travel **to France.**

8 The **last meal** of one 5,000-year-old mummy was goat meat.

9 Ancient Egyptians **mummified animals** such as cats, baboons, and hawks.

10 The site of Puruchuco, near Lima, Peru, contained more than 2,200 **mummies.**

mummy of hawk

Stunning Facts

About

Science

1 **Borborygmus** is the scientific name of the **rumbling sound** your stomach makes when it's **hungry.**

2 A **battery** can be made out of a **potato.**

3 **Humans and slugs** share more than **half of their genes.**

4 A **scatologist** is someone who analyzes **animal poop.**

5 A **storm** on Neptune was as wide as **the entire Earth.**

6 Some **clouds** are more than **10 miles tall.** (16.1 km)

7 You can't really **dig a hole** to China from the U.S.—you'd end up in the **Indian Ocean.**

8 There are **volcanoes** inside glaciers in Iceland.

9 **Chewing gum** can make your heart **beat faster.**

10 Astronomers have **discovered a star** that is made of a **10-billion-trillion-trillion-carat diamond.**

Marvelous

Marsupials

1

A red kangaroo **can leap**
10 feet
(3 m)
in the
air.

2

When a
Tasmanian devil is
scared,
its ears turn bright red.

3

Kangaroos are the
only **large mammals**
that
hop
to get around.

4

Pademelons
thump
their feet
to warn
each other
of danger.

5

A type of **newborn marsupial mouse** is the only mammal that can **breathe** through its skin.

6

Numbats eat up to **20,000** termites a day.

7

Australia is home to the largest number of **marsupials.**

8

Sugar gliders can soar through the air the **length of a football field.**

9

A **wombat's pouch** opens at the **bottom.**

10

The brush-tailed bettong can **pick up things** with **its tail.**

1

The **Roman emperor** Caligula wanted **to make his horse a senator,** according to ancient sources.

2

In ancient India, **surgeons** used ants with clamplike teeth— instead of stitches or staples— to **hold cuts together.**

3

The ancient **Aztec** traded cacao beans as **money.**

Amazing Facts
About the
Ancient World

4

Australian **Aboriginals** —the **world's oldest** living culture—have existed for at least **50,000 years!**

5

Earth is the only planet not named after a **Greek or Roman god.**

6

The ancient **Maya** chewed **gum** made from **tree sap.**

7

Board games were a favorite **pastime** in **ancient Egypt.**

8

Ancient **Egyptians** took up to **70 days** to make a **mummy.**

9

Vikings were mostly **farmers,** not fighters.

10

Tea was originally used as **medicine** in ancient China.

El Castillo Pyramid at Chichén Itza, Mexico

artist's interpretation of the Milky Way

1

It could take up to **8 years** to fly from **Earth to Neptune.**

2

An asteroid called **Cucula** was named after the **cuckoo bird.**

3

From Earth you always look at the **same side** of the moon.

4

The temperature on **Uranus's surface** can plunge to **-357°F** (-216°C).

5

A star at **the center** of the **Crab Nebula** formation rotates **30 times a second.**

Out-of-This-World
Facts About
Space

6

Mars has **blue** sunsets.

7

Astronauts have **grown potatoes** on the **space shuttle.**

8

The north pole of **Uranus** doesn't get sunlight for almost **42 years** at a time.

9

A recent **lightning storm** on Saturn was nearly big enough to cover the **entire United States.**

10

One year on Neptune lasts about **165 Earth years.**

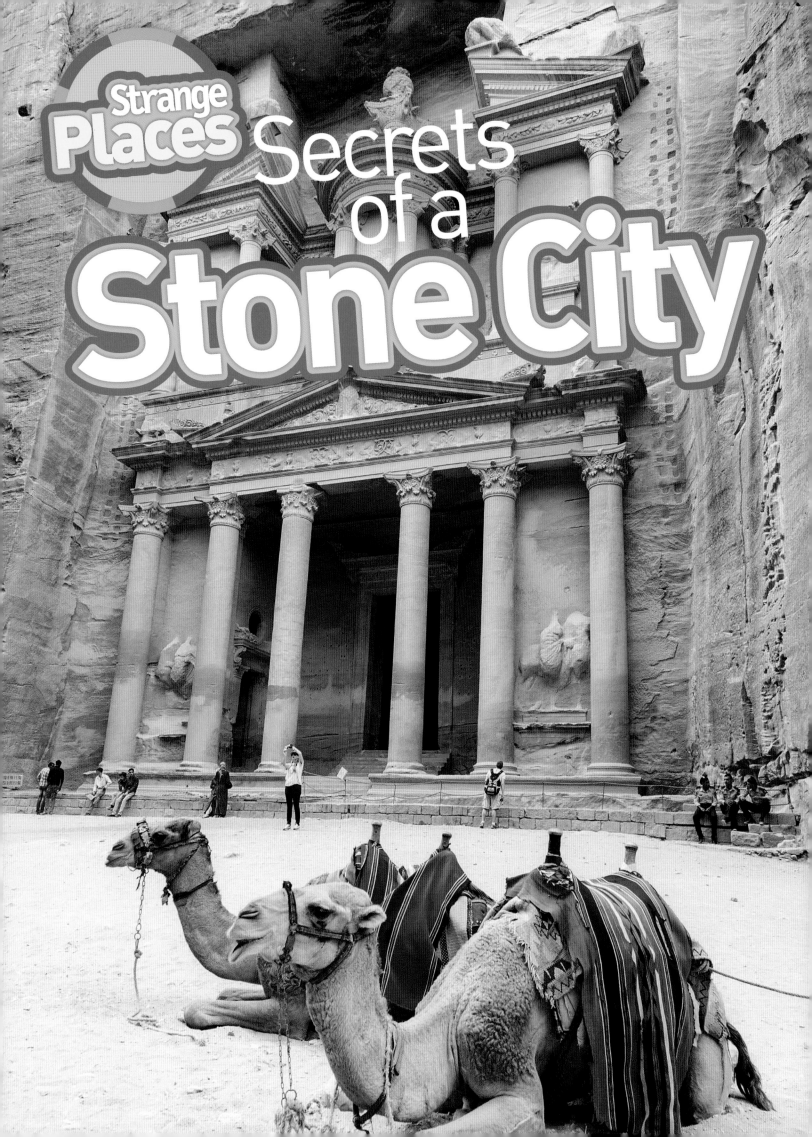

Strange Places

Secrets of a Stone City

How Ancient People Turned a Canyon Into a Town

A desert canyon bakes under the hot sun in southwestern Jordan, a country in the Middle East. From above, the canyon may seem empty. But inside lie the remnants of an ancient city known as Petra (the Greek word for "stone"). Buildings here aren't made of bricks or wood—they're carved right into the towering 300-foot (91-m)-tall canyon walls. How were people able to construct this metropolis without modern equipment? Scientists are digging up clues that could help solve the mystery.

Jordan's King Abdullah II is a former champion **race car driver.**

The **national dish** of Jordan is *mansaf,* chunks of boiled lamb or mutton cooked in a yogurt sauce and served on rice.

SET IN STONE

The area where Petra now sits was settled in the fourth century B.C. by a people called the Nabateans. At first this group lived in goatskin tents. But soon they became wealthy from trading goods such as spices and incense with other communities. Over time they built a lavish city with more than 800 structures that spanned about 20 square miles (51.8 sq km).

Construction workers chiseled temples and tombs, some more than 80 feet (24 m) tall, into the canyon. By the first century, about 30,000 people lived here. In the year 106, the Roman Empire gained control of Petra, and the city lost much of its power. By the seventh century, Petra was largely abandoned.

Hidden from much of the world for centuries, the city became famous after a Swiss adventurer came across the site in 1812. Since then scientists have been trying to solve a puzzle. Many buildings in Petra are several stories high. No one knows how builders were able to carve the sandstone at the top of these structures.

Now Tom Paradise, a geologist, geographer, and cartographer from the University of Arkansas, might have some answers. While studying an unfinished 15-foot (4.6-m)-tall tomb at Petra, he realized that the top of the tomb was carved, but the bottom was untouched. "I wondered if Petra's creators sculpted buildings from top to bottom," he says.

TOMB TWIN

To test his theory, Paradise gathered a team of stone carvers and stonemasons. Their goal was to carve a replica Nabatean tomb out of sandstone from top to bottom. For the experiment, the group used a 15-foot (4.6-m)-tall rock in southern California that resembled the stones of Petra. They worked only with chisels similar to the ones that the Nabateans would've used.

The team soon figured out that they could insert a row of rods into the rock face and lay wooden planks on top to create a working platform. Once one section was done, the platform could be lowered so builders could work on the section below. While they sculpted the rock, the team cut away holes made by the rods, erasing evidence of their use. "It's possible the Nabateans used this method," Paradise says. "And if they did, it explains why no trace of the construction can be seen in Petra."

ROCK ON!

Although Paradise is happy about his team's discoveries, he knows the search for clues isn't over. "Only 5 to 10 percent of Petra has been excavated," Paradise says. "Who knows what else is waiting to be found?" It sounds like the mystery of Petra is still a cliff-hanger.

Flat rock scorpion

1

Giant prickly
stick insects
can release a
defensive smell
that reminds some people of
peanut butter.

2

Scorpions **glow**
under **black light.**

3

The largest known
ant supercolony
stretches nearly
4,000 miles (6,437.4 km)
through **Portugal, Spain,
France, and Italy.**

4

The longest **worms**
can grow to at least a
**hundred
feet.**
(30.5 m)

Crazy Facts

About

Creepy-Crawlies

5

Termite **queens** can lay **6,000 to 7,000** eggs a day.

6

The **Atlas moth** can have up to a **12-inch** (30-cm) wingspan.

7

One of the world's fastest snakes— **the black mamba—** slithers up to **seven miles** an hour. (11 km/h)

8

There's only **one insect** that can survive in **Antarctica:** a tiny wingless fly.

9

More **beetles** live on Earth than any other creature.

10

A male African cicada can make a **sound** as loud as a **power mower.**

Priceless Facts
About
Treasures

1

Most **pirates never buried their loot.**

2

Archaeologists think China's first **emperor's tomb** is probably **full of riches** but nobody's touched it because famous statues of soldiers known as the **terra-cotta army** protect it.

3

A New Mexico, U.S.A., man **buried a treasure** in 2010 worth **$1 million** and **gave hints** in his autobiography, *Thrill of the Chase,* but **no one has found it.**

4

A **cornflake** shaped like the state of Illinois, U.S.A., **sold for $1,350.**

5

A **14-pound pearl**
(6.4-kg)
was found inside a giant clam.

6

The most **expensive ham** in the world is made from Spanish pigs that are fed acorns.

7

There's a **real place** called Treasure Island— it's just northeast of San Francisco.

8

Legend says that if you **lose a tooth** in Mexico, *el ratón* (the mouse) will leave a **treasure under your pillow.**

9

A **gold nugget** found in California weighed a whopping **160 pounds** (72.5 kg) —about as much as **12 bowling balls.**

10

The **Queen of England** has a crown studded with more than **3,000 precious gems.**

1

The modern
cheetah's ancestors
roamed North America
about **four million**
years ago.

2

There are about
**3,000 lightning
flashes**
on Earth
every minute.

3

Nearly **7,000
different languages**
are spoken worldwide.

4

The word
"volcano"
comes from the name of the
Roman fire god,
Vulcan.

5

Earth's temperature
rises slightly during a
full moon.

6

It would take a
stack of more than
100,000 giraffes
to reach the
**outermost layer
of Earth's
atmosphere.**

7

More than a
thousand Earths
could fit inside
Jupiter.

8

The air trapped inside an
iceberg can be
**thousands
of years** old.

9

Humans
have lived on Earth
for about
**200,000 years;
dinosaurs**
walked the planet for roughly
160 million years.

10

It would take nearly three days and nights to reach Earth's core if you traveled **65 miles an hour** (104.6 km/h) straight into the ground.

Earthshaking Facts About Geology

1
Some bees may
sleep on flowers.

2
A bee **beats its**
wings
up to **12,000 times**
each minute.

3
Bees have a **stomach**
for carrying
nectar.

4
Sweat bees
like the taste of
human
perspiration.

5
Beeswax
is **often used** on
tambourines.

6
The alkali bee
can visit up to
6,000 flowers per day.

Bee Facts to Buzz About

7 Utah, U.S.A., is known as the Beehive State.

8 Ancient Greeks used bee venom to treat baldness.

9 In summer, a single hive can house up to 80,000 honeybees.

10 A honeybee would have to travel the equivalent of 2 times around the Earth to gather enough nectar for 1 pound (453 g) of honey.

Fun Facts to Unwrap About Winter Holidays

1

One of the most popular Hanukkah treats is *sufganiyot,* or **jelly-filled doughnuts.**

2

The U.S. Postal Service collects **millions of letters** written to **Santa** every year.

3

The world's largest **menorah—** a candelabra used during Hanukkah—was taller than a **three-story building.**

4

The word **Kwanzaa** comes from a phrase meaning **"first fruits"** in an African language called Swahili.

5 The record-holder at the **Great Fruitcake Toss** in Colorado, U.S.A., flung a leftover fruitcake **1,500 feet** (457.2 m) with a catapult.

6 A survey found that about **half of dog and cat owners** in the United States **buy holiday gifts** for their pets.

7 *Apollo 8,* the first manned spacecraft to **circle the moon,** entered orbit on **Christmas Eve** in 1968.

8 Many cities hold **community bonfires** to **burn** Christmas trees after December 25.

9 The biggest **gingerbread house** was made with **7,200 eggs** and **1,800 pounds of butter** (2,155 kg)

10 A **165-year-old holiday card** was auctioned off for nearly **$40,000** in 2001.

DUDE STOMPS CITY

WHAT City diorama

WHERE Moscow, Russia

DETAILS This guy better watch where he steps. Some 300 workers created this 60-foot (18.3-m)-wide, mostly plastic model of the Russian capital. The diorama traveled the world as part of a road show celebrating the country's history. The mini-Moscow even comes equipped with daytime and nighttime lighting. What, no traffic?

Extreme Weirdness

RUNNERS TURN GREEN

WHAT Running sculptures

WHERE Liverpool, England

DETAILS Talk about going nowhere fast. This athletic-themed installation, dubbed "The Runner," was one of several pieces in a citywide art festival. Situated above a parking garage, the sprinters honor Liverpool's past Olympic contenders. On your mark, get set, go!

FLOATING PINK MOUSE

WHAT Inflatable rodent

WHERE Lyon, France

DETAILS No way this guy is fitting through a mousehole. It's 64 times bigger than an average mouse—and it's inflatable. The 32-foot (9.75-m)-long, 16-foot (4.9-m)-wide pink mouse floated in the Rhône River to promote flood awareness. Is there a giant piece of cheese nearby?

JUMBO-SIZE JACK-O'-LANTERN

WHAT Halloween light display

WHERE Vancouver, Canada

DETAILS This is one pumpkin that won't rot. Science World, an interactive science museum, transformed itself into a huge jack-o'-lantern in honor of Halloween. Every few seconds the orange and green lights lit up on different spots around the building so people could see them from all over the city. We can't wait to see what they do for Thanksgiving.

ATTACK OF THE COMB

WHAT Weird haircuts

WHERE Changsha, China

DETAILS Answer carefully if you're ever asked if you want a free haircut. A pair of hair-stylists offered complimentary trims to city residents. But their styling tools were a three-foot (1-m)-long comb and oversize scissors! One brave volunteer had her hair snipped in front of a crowd. That new do definitely wasn't a don't.

SHARK ON LAND!

WHAT Braderie de Lille

WHERE Lille, France

DETAILS Ever seen a strolling great white? A shark-shaped headpiece is one of thousands of quirky purchases you can make at Braderie de Lille, or the street market of Lille. The event, Europe's biggest flea market, welcomes some two million visitors every September and dates back to the 12th century. The real sharks here are the bargain hunters.

GIANT ANTS INVADE

WHAT Art installation

WHERE Bogotá, Colombia

DETAILS Quick—call the exterminator! Some 1,300 big ants were seen along the side of several public buildings in this South American city. But the nearly two-foot (61-cm)-long insects aren't the real deal. A local artist created the creepy-crawlies from glass fiber and used cotton to tie the separate body pieces together. Still, we'll have our picnic elsewhere.

107

Deep Facts

About

Caves

1
Certain **ice caves** in Iceland are filled with **hot springs.**

2
Cave bears, which are now extinct, weighed around **1,500 pounds.** (680 kg)

3
1,000-year-old **popcorn** was found in a **Utah cave.**

4
Caves can be formed by **earthquakes.**

5
Some doctors in the 1800s thought cave air could **cure illness.**

6
Ancient **cave paintings** in Australia show an almost **8-foot** (2.4-m) **-tall bird.**

7

Many cave-dwelling fish **don't have eyes.**

8

Icicle-shaped cave formations called **stalactites** and **stalagmites** grow super slow— less than **0.04 inches** per year. (0.1 cm)

9

In Thailand, a rare species of cave fish **walks up waterfalls** like a lizard.

10

Scientists have found signs of **ancient wildfires** by **studying** caves.

Frrr-ozen

Facts to
Chill You Out

1

Antarctica is a desert, even though it's covered mostly in ice.

2

A man in New England, U.S.A., **invented ice cubes** by **harvesting ice** and shipping it to hotter countries.

3

Melting glaciers and icebergs make a fizzy sound called "bergy seltzer" or "ice sizzle."

5

You can call home from an **ice telephone booth** at a festival in **Alaska**.

4

Small icebergs are called "growlers" and "bergy bits."

6

There have been **five major ice ages** in Earth's history.

7

An Inca woman **frozen in ice** for more than 500 years looks just as she did when she died—the ice even preserved the lice in her hair.

8

The largest **smoothie** on record was **824 gallons** (3,119.2 L)—enough to fill about **20 bathtubs.**

9

8,962 people made **snow angels** at the same time on the grounds of the North Dakota State Capitol, U.S.A.

10

Nomads created **ice skates** made of bone at least **4,000 years ago.**

111

Rad Facts

About
Rodents

3 Scientists **can grow a human ear on the back of a rat.**

4 Gerbils can recognize each other by the **taste of their saliva.**

2 In Switzerland, it's **ilegal to own just one guinea pig— you must have at least two.**

5 A gerbil may **stomp its feet to communicate.**

1 Guinea pigs often **sleep with their eyes open.**

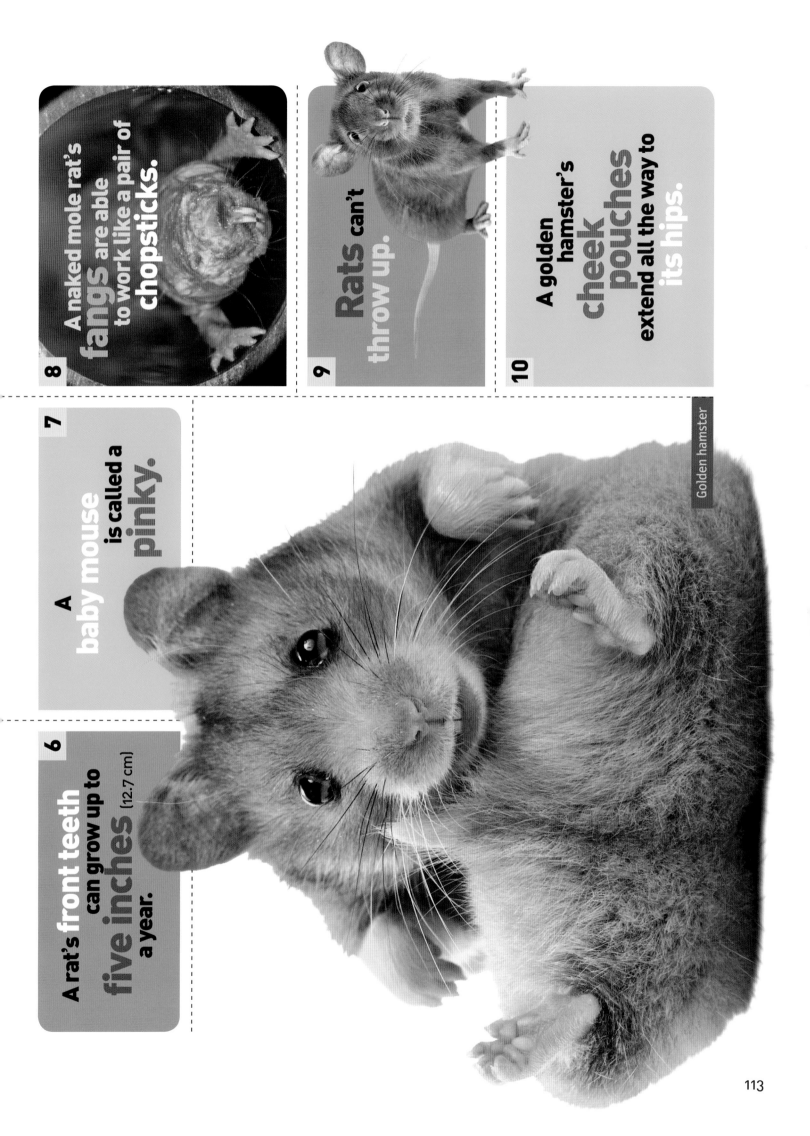

8 A naked mole rat's **fangs** are able to work like a pair of **chopsticks.**

9 **Rats can't** throw up.

10 A golden hamster's **cheek pouches** extend all the way to its hips.

7 A baby mouse is called a **pinky.**

6 A rat's front teeth can grow up to **five inches** (12.7 cm) a year.

Golden hamster

1

Some **giant jellyfish** have **tentacles** that could stretch one-third the length of a **football field.**

2

The **world's smallest seahorse** is smaller than a postage stamp.

3

Sea otters stash food between rolls of skin.

4

Up to **40 orcas** hunt in one group.

5

The tentacles of a **lion's mane jellyfish** can stretch more than **100 feet** (30.5 m).

6

Sharks lived on Earth more than **170 million years** before dinosaurs.

7

An **octopus** can have nearly **2,000 suckers** on its arms.

8

Male walruses make a **bell-like** sound to **attract mates.**

9

A female **ocean sunfish** may spawn **300 million eggs** at a time.

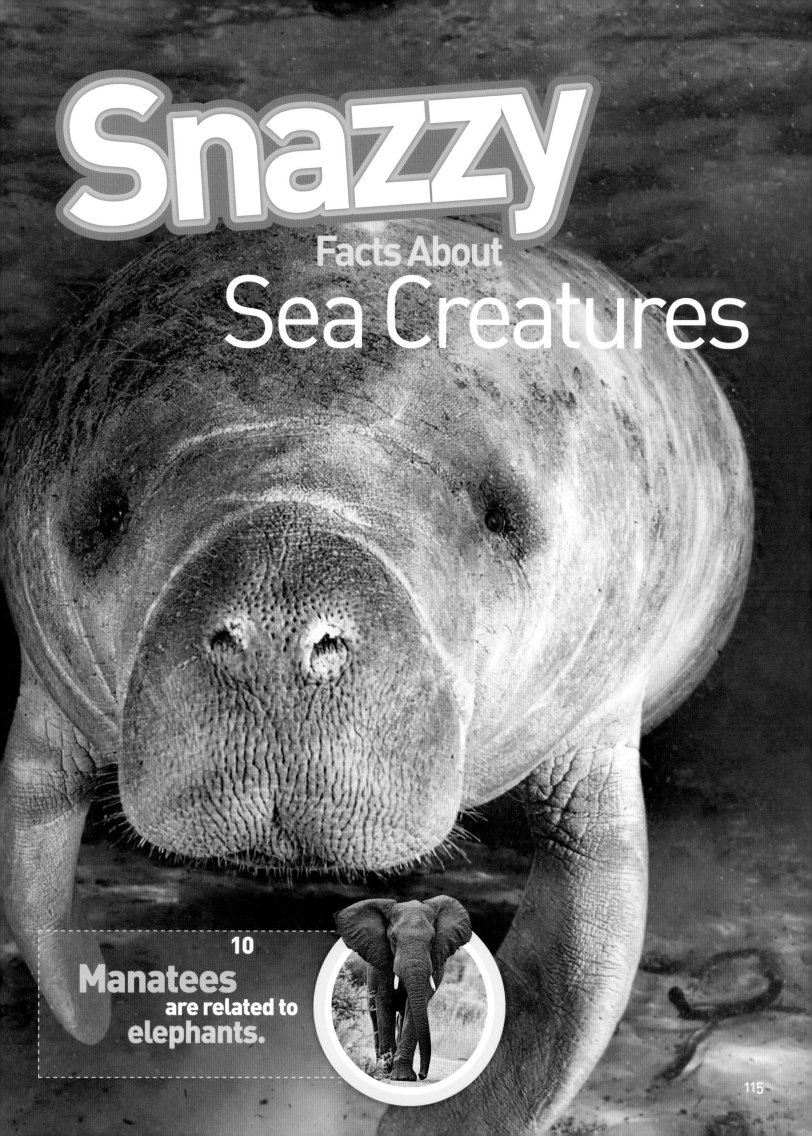

Snazzy
Facts About
Sea Creatures

10
Manatees are related to **elephants.**

Daring

Dining

1

Fried scorpions
on skewers are a **popular snack** in Beijing, China.

2

Peanut butter
is hard to find outside the U.S.—many people in other countries don't like the taste.

3

A company in Seattle, Washington, U.S.A., once sold **bacon-flavored soda.**

4

Cute animals commonly eaten in foreign countries include **puffins** in Iceland, guinea pigs in Peru, and **kangaroos** in Australia.

5 The **bhut jolokia pepper** from India can be **400 times spicier** than Tabasco sauce.

6 When incorrectly prepared, **cassava**—a plant originating in South America—can produce **deadly poison.**

7 A **piecaken** is a **pie** baked inside a **cake.**

8 In Poland, you can try **cold fruit soup** with pasta.

9 A type of coffee is made from beans **ingested and excreted** by a mammal called the Asian palm civet.

10 In other countries, Pringles **makes chips** flavored like **fish ball, prawn, roast turkey, and blueberry hazelnut.**

1

Weighing less than a penny, **bumblebee bats** are the smallest living mammals.

2

The fastest **swimming bird,** a gentoo penguin, glides through water at 22 miles an hour. (35 km/h)

3

Bears are thought to have the best sense of smell and can follow a scent for miles— black bears up to 20 miles (32.2 km), and polar bears **twice that!**

4

The **woolliest** sheep was found with seven years' worth— or about **90 pounds** (40.8 kg) of wool.

5

Wild giraffes sleep about a **half hour a day,** the shortest amount of any animal.

Record-Breakers

That Rock

6

The world's smallest **chameleon** can perch on a matchstick head.

7

A bird called the **arctic tern** makes the farthest **yearly migration:** about **25,000 miles** (40,233 km).

8

The **most venomous** snake is the *Oxyuranus microlepidotus*, which is nicknamed the "fierce snake" for its **cocktail of poison** that **paralyzes** victims, **damages** their muscles, and makes it **hard to breathe.**

9

The **eye** of the **colossal squid** is a record-breaking **10.6 inches** across. (26.9 cm)

10

Saltwater crocodiles, the biggest living reptiles, can grow **longer** than **6 baseball bats.**

Facts You Can CountOn

1 Every day, **70,000 puppies** and **kittens** are born in the United States.

2 Americans eat approximately **250 eggs per person** per year.

3 A man in India **recited from memory 70,000 decimal places** of the number pi— it took him almost **10 hours.**

4 About **8 billion candy hearts** are produced each year.

5

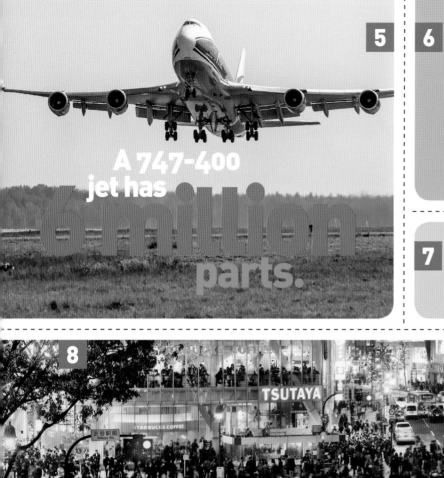

A 747-400 jet has **6 million parts.**

6

Today's fastest **passenger train** travels at a max speed of **267 miles an hour** (430 km/h).

7

The **oldest koi** fish lived to be **226 years old.**

8

At Japan's Shibuya crosswalk, the **busiest pedestrian crossing** in the world, **2,500 people** cross the street at the same time.

9

About **1,000 grains** of salt are in a **pinch.**

10

LEGO has made more than **600 billion** toy bricks since 1958.

1
There are **pyramids** in Sudan that rival Egypt's—the tallest stands about **100 feet** (30.5 km) **high.**

2
Mummified crocodiles have been discovered in ancient Egyptian cemeteries.

3
The **Sahara desert** is about as big as the United States.

4
More than a **thousand languages** are spoken in Africa.

5
Africa's Arabian camels have one hump; Bactrian camels in Asia **have two.**

6
Some scenes in the *Star Wars* movies were filmed in Tunisia.

Astounding
Facts About
Africa

7

In Ethiopia, **the day starts** at sunrise (6 a.m.) instead of **midnight.**

8

From the southern Spanish coast, you can actually **see Morocco—** it's only **9 miles** (14.5 km) between continents.

9

Tanzania has the world's largest population of **tree-climbing lions.**

10

Thrill-seeking tourists **sandboard** down **giant dunes** on many of Africa's beaches and deserts.

African Lion

1

A whale shark's mouth is almost as wide as a car.

2

Greenland shark meat is considered a delicacy in Iceland and Greenland, but it takes about five months to prepare—otherwise, the meat is poisonous.

3

A shortfin mako shark can leap higher than a giraffe's head.

4

Some sharks can swim the length of a soccer field in five seconds.

5

A few of the **weirdest** things that have been found in shark stomachs: license plates, tires, reindeer, rubber boots, and dolls.

6

A spiny dogfish shark can live more than 100 years.

7

The **cookiecutter shark** was given its name for the way it takes chunks out of its prey.

8

Shark teeth can't get **cavities.**

10

The **great white shark** has the **largest teeth** of any living shark.

9

Some sharks can smell blood about **half a mile** (0.8 km) **away.**

Surprising
Facts About
Sharks

CRATER VS. CANYON

Just like your skin can reveal scars and wrinkles over time, the Earth's surface tells a story about its past. Two of these visible markers are craters and canyons. What's the difference? A crater is an area that has been hollowed out by a fast-moving meteor hitting it hard or by an explosion of some kind (as is the case with the craters at the top of volcanoes). Even though craters are generally big, they aren't always obvious! It's sometimes hard to spot them—weather makes the edges of the crater a little fuzzy over time, and they could also be covered in plant life. While craters are fairly shallow, canyons are deep valleys with steep sides, most famously shown by the Grand Canyon. The Grand Canyon and similar canyons were made by rivers cutting through the Earth over millions of years. But the Earth's tectonic plates shifting over time can also cause canyons. Earth isn't the only planet covered in both craters and canyons—Mars, Venus, and Mercury have plenty, too!

What's the Difference?

Check out these similar pairings and see how you can determine this from that!

MONKEY VS. APE

If you're at the zoo and want an easy way to tell your primates apart, here's a very visible clue: Monkeys have tails, apes don't. And the differences don't end there. Apes (gorillas, chimpanzees, orangutans, etc.) are bigger and smarter, with the ability to communicate with one another (and people!) and even use tools. They also tend to have fairly long life spans (35-50 years, depending on the species). Monkeys (like baboons, macaques, and tamarins) tend to have a more noticeable snout and rely on smell more than sight. They are smaller in stature and some species live only 10 to 15 years in the wild. Apes and monkeys—along with their smaller primate buddies the prosimians— can both be found in Africa and Asia, but you'll find only monkeys swinging through the trees of South and Central America. Don't be surprised if you see the chimps studying you at the zoo—humans and chimpanzees share as much as 99 percent of the same DNA!

TURTLE VS. TORTOISE

Prepare to be shell-shocked: Tortoise and turtle are not simply two names for the same slowpoke. The two reptiles look similar, but turtles are mostly swimmers, with fins and a sleek shell shape to prove it. Tortoises, on the other hand, are land dwellers with a sturdier, rounder shell and long claws better suited for digging. (They can also tuck their heads completely inside their shells, while turtles cannot.) Dinnertime means a mix of plant life for tortoises, but turtles are hungry omnivores that eat their veggies alongside insects and small fish. Forget the hare—if these two were racing, turtles would definitely win, as long as it happened in the water. They're much faster swimmers than tortoises are walkers!

MACARON VS. MACAROON

In the world of sweets, everyone's talking about the macaron—a delicate little sandwich cookie that's recently made its way west from France and comes in bright colors and a variety of flavors. However, many Americans pronounce "macaron" as "macaroon," as in, rhymes with "spoon." But a macaroon is an entirely different cookie: a small, sweet ball of shredded coconut sometimes dipped in chocolate. So why the single "o" separating them? Historically, macarons and macaroons were born from the same almond-based cookie and the same Italian word: *maccherone,* which means "fine paste" (and also led to macaroni). The French started to fill their cookies with chocolate or jam; Americans swapped the almond for coconut in the late 1800s. The result: both delicious!

VENOMOUS VS. POISONOUS

Let's get one thing straight: When you're talking about animals and insects, it's best to stay as far away as possible from both venomous and poisonous ones. And while people often mistakenly use the words interchangeably, they definitely don't mean the same thing! Inside your body, venom and poison can cause similar symptoms, ranging from mild pain to (eek!) death—one is not necessarily more dangerous than the other. The difference lies in the way they make contact. Venomous creatures (many kinds of snakes, spiders, and scorpions, all octopuses, and a few others) use a stinger or fangs to strike their enemies, usually as self-defense. Poisonous creatures (lots of frogs, plus some butterflies, a few types of birds, and the spiky pufferfish) simply have to be touched or eaten, depending on the animal, to be toxic. But understandably, poisonous beasts don't want to be eaten— they generally are brightly colored or have another way (like how the pufferfish blows up like a ball) to alert predators to keep their distance. Thanks for the warning!

JAM VS. JELLY

When it comes to your lunchtime sandwich, which J do you prefer slathered next to the PB? Jam and jelly are fruit preserves that sit side by side in grocery aisles, and for good reason—they're virtually identical and used for similar purposes (mostly, to keep peanut butter from getting lonely). Jam and jelly both rely on something called pectin to make them thick and gel-like. Jam is chunky because it is made by cooking down whole fruit and sugar, using the natural pectin of the fruit to thicken it. Smooth, clear jelly, however, uses only fruit juice and sugar, so powdered pectin has to be added to set it. Both make a pretty great sandwich!

1

Franklin D. **Roosevelt** set a record for keeping the **most dogs—** 11!—at the White House.

2

George **Washington** had a set of **false teeth** made from **hippo tusks.**

3

Richard M. **Nixon** once telephoned **astronauts** on the **moon.**

4

There's a portrait of Ronald **Reagan** made from about **10,000 jelly beans.**

Stately
Facts About
U.S.
Presidents

5 Ulysses S. **Grant** was fined for **speeding** down a Washington, D.C., street in a **horse-drawn carriage.**

6 James **Garfield** could write **Latin** with one hand and **Greek** with the other **at the same time.**

7 President Barack **Obama** appeared in a 2009 **Spider-Man** comic book.

8 Calvin **Coolidge's** wife had a **pet raccoon** named Rebecca.

9 Gerald R. **Ford** held his daughter's **high school prom** at the White House.

10 An 11-year-old girl asked Abraham **Lincoln** to grow his **famous beard.**

Facts About  Wild Cats

That Are Claw-Some

1

Each species of **big cat** has a **unique** **coat** for camouflage.

2

The **Bengal tiger** is India's national animal.

3

A **leopard** can drag a small antelope up a **50-foot** (15-m) **tree.**

A big cat's **sense of smell** is 20 times stronger than a human's.

4
A **serval's big ears** help it hear the soft sounds of scurrying **prey.**

5
Snow leopards can leap as far as **45 feet** (13.7 m)— the length of a humpback whale!

7
There are nearly **40 species** of wild cats in the world.

8
A puma is also called a **mountain lion,** a **panther,** and a **cougar.**

9
A **cheetah** can accelerate **faster** than a **race car.**

10
Cats see **six times better** at night than humans.

1

Castle stairways usually go up **clockwise,** so people **defending the castle** could come down carrying **swords** in their right hands.

2

The castle **barber** was also the **dentist.**

3

Disneyland U.S.A.'s **Sleeping Beauty Castle** was inspired by **Neuschwanstein** Castle in Germany.

Cool Facts
About
Castles

Neuschwanstein Castle

4

Ireland's **Blarney Castle** has a stone that **visitors kiss** for **good luck.**

5

England's **Windsor Castle** is about **200 times larger** than a typical U.S. house.

6

The number of **people who lived** in some castles could fill a **small village.**

7

The **medieval** version of a **toilet** was called a **garderobe,** a hole that sometimes led waste out **to the moat.**

8

Supplies were often **smuggled** into castles through **secret tunnels.**

9

The **first castles** were built around a **thousand years** ago.

10

The world's **oldest football** (or American soccer ball) was found at Scotland's Stirling Castle, where **kings and queens** could have **played with it.**

It would take more than 1,500 human hearts to equal the weight of a blue whale's heart.

Icky Facts to
Creep
You Out

1

Cat urine
can glow under
black
light.

2

"corpse
flower"
grows up to 12 feet (3.7 m)
tall and smells like
rotting meat.

3

Up to
a third of
your
pillow's
weight
is likely dead skin,
bugs, mites,
and their poop.

4

Phasmaphobia
is the fear of ghosts.

In ancient Egypt, **mummies' brains** were removed **through the nose.**

6

5 A man sculpted a **statue of himself** using **his own** hair, teeth, and nails.

7 **Your food** travels about **30 feet** (9.1 m) **from the time it goes in your mouth to the time you go to the bathroom.**

8 In 2004, a Turkish man set a record for **sucking milk in** through his nose and **squirting it out** of his eye the farthest.

9 **Mike the chicken** set a world record for living for 18 months **without a head,** from 1945 to 1947.

10 One **coffin** was designed to look like a **lobster.**

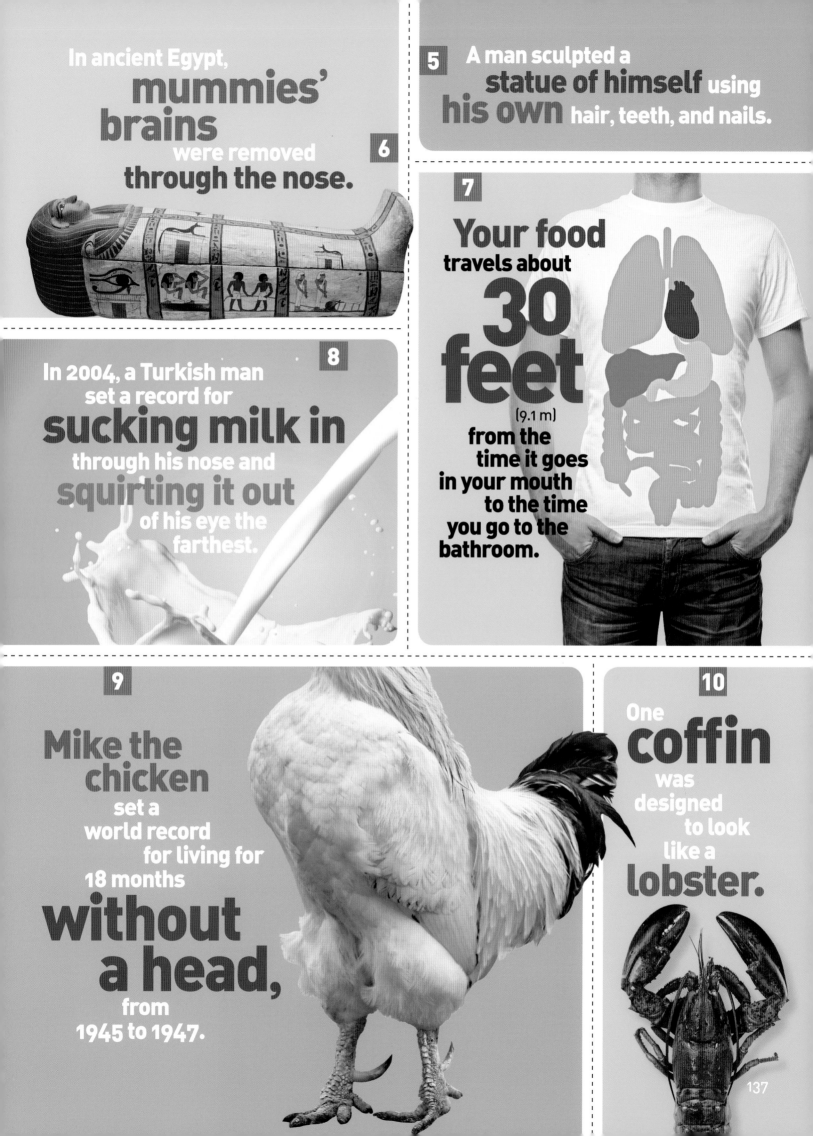

Facts to Light Up Your World

1

Light from the sun reaches Earth in **8.32 minutes;** the space shuttle would take about **220 days.**

2

The first lighthouse was **three times taller** than most ones today.

3

Lemons can power **lightbulbs.**

4

Some jellyfish **give off light** to scare away predators.

5

If you combined **all the colors** of the sky, you'd get a beige color known as **"cosmic latte."**

6

Lightning
flashes
more than
44 times
each second
all over the world.

7

A Ferris wheel
in California runs on
solar power.

8

Bees see
color in **ultraviolet** light.

9

A New Year's
celebration in
Portugal
included more than
65,000
fireworks.

10

Antarctica can have
24 hours
of daylight
in summer.

Awesome Facts About
Animals in the Americas

1 A mobula ray's **wingspan** can be **10 feet** (3 m) across.

2 A group of **Pacific parakeets** in Nicaragua makes its home **in an active volcano.**

3 Some scientists think **spider monkeys** eat **dirt** to help them **digest.**

4 **Bighorn rams** can **crash** into each other at **20 miles an hour.** (32.2 km/h)

5

Some **flamingos** live in the **chilly** Andes Mountains.

7

Jaguar jaws are **strong enough** to crack open **tortoise shells.**

9

Mustangs may eat **15 pounds** (6.8 kg) of food a day— equal to about **70 burgers.**

6

Certain **alligators bellow** loud enough to **shake** nearby objects.

8

Northern grasshopper mice **howl** when **defending** their territory.

10

The **tube-lipped** nectar bat's **tongue** is longer than its body.

Bighorn rams

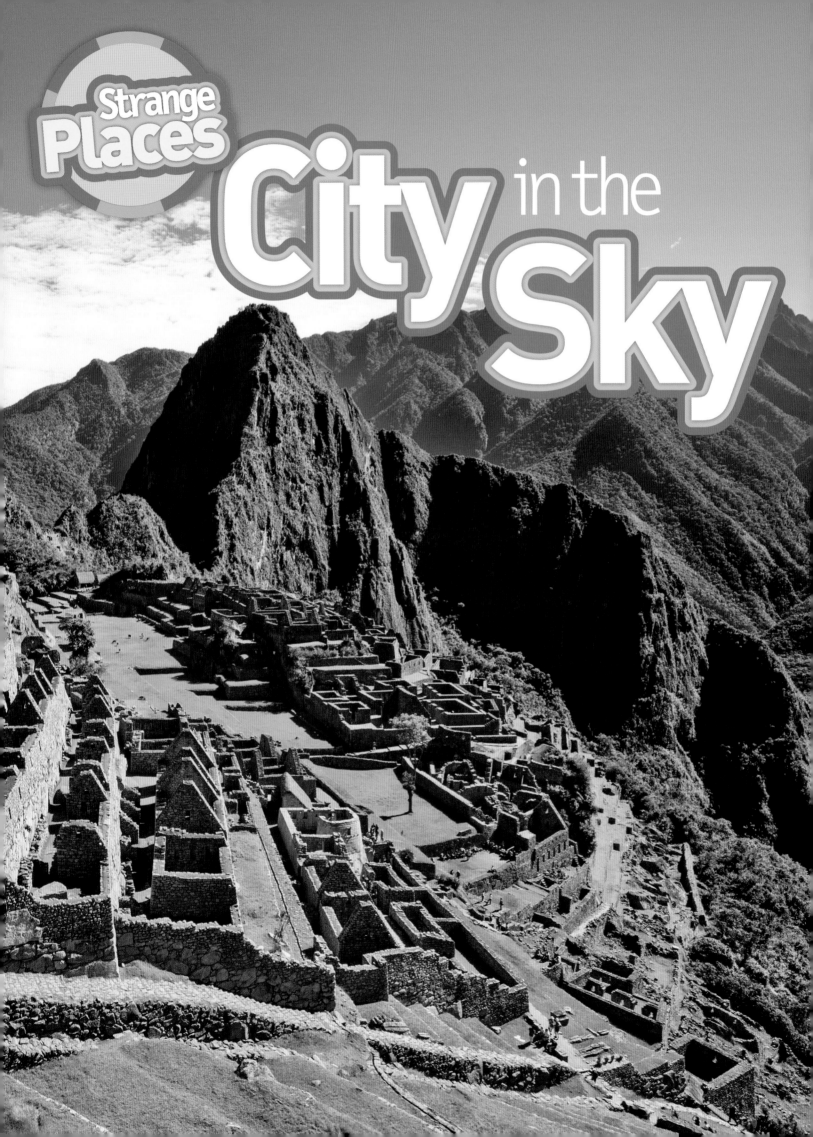

Strange Places

City in the Sky

Scientists search for clues about why the community of Machu Picchu was built.

The peaks of the Andes mountain range in Peru stretch for miles in every direction, their summits wrapped in mist. As the sun rises in the sky, the mist burns away, revealing an unexpected sight. Perched nearly 8,000 feet (2,438 m) high on one of the mountaintops is an old city made of stone. Known as Machu Picchu (or "Old Peak" in the local language of Quechua), the site has been here for centuries. But not even the descendants of the builders who live near Machu Picchu know for sure why the city was built.

THE RISE OF MACHU PICCHU

Machu Picchu was constructed some 500 years ago during the Inca Empire. This powerful civilization thrived during the 15th and 16th centuries, ruling parts of western South America. Archaeologists believe that it took hundreds of builders to construct the mountaintop city, which was a five-day trek from the empire's capital. Using stones from an on-site quarry, they made houses, temples, and even fountains. They also built more than a hundred stone staircases to connect different levels in and around the city. But after the Inca Empire fell in the mid-1500s, Machu Picchu was abandoned.

Few knew about the neglected metropolis until an American explorer stumbled upon its ruins in July 1911. As news of his discovery spread around the world, so did theories about the mysterious sky-high city. Many people thought Machu Picchu was a fortress where the Inca battled invaders. Some have even suggested that aliens built it to have a base on planet Earth. (Yeah, not likely.) Recently, scientists digging for clues about the purpose of Machu Picchu have made some interesting finds.

LOVE OF THE LAND

Anthropologist and National Geographic Explorer-in-Residence Johan Reinhard thinks answers to the Machu Picchu puzzle lie in the surrounding landscape. "The Inca believed that gods lived in landforms and bodies of water," Reinhard says. "And they worshipped these sites."

During one expedition to Machu Picchu, Reinhard came across several large stones carved into the shape of the surrounding peaks. "The carvings were likely made to celebrate these landforms," Reinhard says. "The mountains were considered sacred, and the stones reflect that." Reinhard also knew that the peak that Machu Picchu rests on is encircled by a river the Inca worshipped. "The area was important to the Inca," Reinhard says. "And Machu Picchu may have been built to honor this cherished landscape where mighty gods were thought to dwell."

STAR POWER

It's likely that the site was also a gathering place during astronomical events such as the summer and winter solstices (the longest and shortest days of the year). Machu Picchu's high elevation makes it a perfect spot for sky-watching. And celestial events were important to the Inca, even affecting how buildings here were designed. For instance, one temple in the city was built at an angle so that the sun shines directly into its window on the morning of the winter solstice, illuminating a stone shrine.

In 2013, a team of archaeologists from Peru and Poland found even more evidence that Machu Picchu was used as a viewing spot for celestial events. The scientists were examining an unexcavated section of Machu Picchu when they uncovered a building that was likely an astronomical observatory where Inca priests may have plotted the movement of stars and planets.

So are the mysteries of Machu Picchu solved? Not quite. Evidence certainly exists that the site was built to honor sacred land and used as an astronomical observatory. But without written records—or a time machine to travel back and question the Inca—we may never be absolutely sure. In other words, the purpose of this city in the sky may forever stay cloudy.

An estimated **60 percent** of Peru is covered in **rain forest.**

Peru's Colca Canyon is nearly **twice as deep** as the **Grand Canyon.**

Purr-fect Facts

About Cats

1 Some cats are **allergic to people.**

2 Adult cats **only meow** to communicate **with people,** not other cats.

3 A litter of kittens is also called a **kindle.**

4 **Catnip** can affect **lions** and **tigers.**

5 People in the United States own about **88 million cats** and **75 million dogs.**

6 **Felix** the cat was the **first balloon** in the Macy's Thanksgiving Day Parade.

7

Some experts believe cats **were domesticated** at least **8,000 years** ago in Egypt.

8

Cats **communicate** using at least **26 known "cat words."**

9

All cats are born with **blue eyes.**

10

A cat named Stubbs is the **honorary mayor** of Talkeetna, Alaska.

Surprising Facts About Spiders

1
There are **more than 40,000 species** of spiders.

2

Golden silk orb-weaver spiders vibrate their webs to **distract predators.**

3
After a **large meal,** a tarantula may not eat for a month.

4
A pound (453 g) of **spider silk** could stretch **around the** Equator.

5 The oldest known **spider fossils** are more than **300 million years** old.

6 Black widow spiders are **more poisonous** than rattlesnakes.

7 A **real spider** inspired the book *Charlotte's Web.*

9 Crab spiders **change color** to blend in with their surroundings.

8 In Australia, colonies of **baby spiders** appear to rain down from the sky around May and August, covering everything in silky webs.

10 A spider **eats** about **2,000 insects** a year.

1

Blue whales are the **largest animals that ever lived.** They're even bigger than **most dinosaurs!**

2

The world's **longest mountain range** is **under the sea.**

3

A swordfish **can swim** about **as fast** as a **cheetah** can run.

Splashy Facts to Dive Into!

4

Scuba divers **can send postcards** from a **mailbox** off the coast of Japan that's nearly **33 feet** (10 m) **underwater.**

5

The **leafy seadragon** has **plant-looking fins** that help it **camouflage** as **seaweed.**

6

Cockroaches can **survive underwater** for **up to 15 minutes.**

7

Earth has the **same amount of water** today as it did **100 million** years ago.

8

Cuvier's **beaked whales** are the **deepest-diving** mammals— they can stay underwater for more than **two hours.**

9

It would take a **stack** of more than **nine Empire State Buildings** to equal the average **depth of the ocean.**

10

Porcupines can **float.**

1

Ghost bats
may be named for their translucent wings and **ghostlike color.**

2

A **Kitti's hog-nosed bat** **weighs** about the same as **a dime.**

3

The **pallid bat is** **immune** to scorpion **venom.**

4

The Malaysian **flying fox's** **wingspan** stretches **up to 6 feet.** (1.8 m)

5

Bat **hibernation caves** are called **hibernacula.**

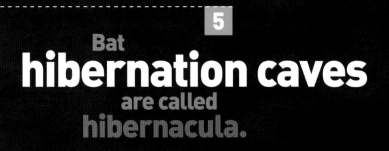
Little brown bat

Fab Facts
About
Bats

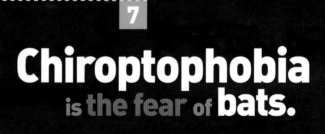

Lesser horseshoe bat

6

Bat guano (poop) was once **Texas, U.S.A.'s** biggest natural export.

8

The Spotted bat's **ears** are almost as long **as its body.**

10

Some bats **can live** for **30** years.

7

Chiroptophobia is the fear of **bats.**

9

Certain bats **can eat** more than **500 mosquitoes** in an hour.

Festive Facts About
Holidays
Around the World

1

Each year on October 9, **South Koreans** celebrate **their alphabet.**

2

In Japan, the most popular **Christmas meal** comes from **Kentucky Fried Chicken.**

3

On **Indonesia's Independence Day,** people climb greased poles for **prizes.**

4

A **gigantic 4,000-pound** (1,814-kg) **menorah** is lit in **New York City** during Hanukkah.

5

Children in Sweden **dress as witches and collect candy** the Thursday before **Easter.**

December 23 is the Night of the Radishes in Oaxaca, Mexico. 6

7 **Turkmenistan observes a holiday that honors the country's melons.**

8 **Women give chocolates to men on Valentine's Day in Japan; then on White Day, March 14, men are expected to give the ladies a gift.**

9 **Every Christmas Eve, a man dressed as Santa water-skis on a river in Virginia, U.S.A.**

10 **On April Fools' Day, Italian kids put cutouts of paper fish on the backs of their friends.**

1

A **housefly** can **turn somersaults** in **the air.**

2

Mosquitoes prefer to bite people who have **smelly feet.**

3

Dragonflies appeared on Earth 140 million years **before** the first **birds.**

4

Tiny bugs called **mites** live in our **eyebrows.**

Facts to Bug Out You

5 Raw **termites** taste like **pineapple.**

6 A **praying mantis** has only **one ear.**

7 Most **female fireflies** can't **fly.**

8 Some **young spiders** can **regrow lost legs.**

9 Giant **water bugs**— which can grow to be more than **two inches** (5 cm) **long**— have been known to eat **small frogs.**

10 Whirligig beetles have **two** pairs of eyes— one pair for looking **underwater** and one for looking **above water.**

ONE-WHEELED WONDER

WHAT Extra-large unicycle

WHERE Beijing, China

DETAILS Watch your balance! Inventor Li Yongli does just that when he rides this giant unicycle. He calls the six-and-a-half-foot (2-m) pedal-powered cycle—one of many he has built—the number one vehicle in the world. It's definitely one of the most interesting!

Extreme Weirdness

HAT FOR BREAKFAST

WHAT English breakfast hat

WHERE Ascot, England

DETAILS Some people wear their pride on their sleeve—this fashionable woman wears hers on her hat. British patriotism is big at Royal Ascot, an English horse-racing event held every June. Among the hats worn by the crowd was this English breakfast: bacon, sausages, tomatoes, eggs, mushrooms, and beans. Wonder if she's willing to share.

PHONE GROWS BRAIN

WHAT Brain-shaped phone booth

WHERE São Paulo, Brazil

DETAILS Need a little extra brainpower? This brain-shaped phone booth was part of a design competition. A hundred designs—including a disco ball, a ladybug, an ear, and a clown—were installed over public telephones in Brazil's largest city. Cell phones have never seemed so boring.

SHAGGY SCULPTURE

WHAT Grass dog

WHERE Hamamatsu, Japan

DETAILS Pet this pup and you might get grass stains. Made out of plants, the six-foot (1.8-m)-tall dog was an entry in an international Mosaiculture contest. Artists combine plants and wire frames to create large, three-dimensional sculptures. Other entries included a volcano and a dragonfly. Hope the artists remembered to water their creations.

WATER FAUCET FLOATS

WHAT Suspended water tap

WHERE Ypres, Belgium

DETAILS What's the trick to this floating faucet? A clear pipe inside the falling water creates the illusion. The supportive pipe carries water from a pool on the ground to the rear of the faucet. The water loops around and is spewed back out into the pool. That's why it looks like a never-ending flow of water. Now we're thirsty.

SWANS TAKE BOAT RIDE

WHAT Swan roundup

WHERE Hamburg, Germany

DETAILS This is one weird water taxi. Every fall before the water gets too cold, swans living on the Alster River are gathered into boats and driven to a nearby ice-free pond. In the spring, they'll return to their warm-weather waters. These birds are swimming on easy street.

Halloween

Facts How to Howl About

1 Rumor has it that **the ghost** of a **British soldier** haunts the **White House.**

2 More than **35 million pounds** of **candy corn** (15,875,732 kg) are produced each year in the U.S.— that's the weight of **101 jumbo jets.**

3

Competitors
race coffins
down the
main street
of a Colorado town
every October.

4

Pumpkins
and witches
are the
most
popular
Halloween
costumes
for pets.

5

Prehistoric people
believed that
**spirits
live in trees.**

6

The word
"pumpkin"
comes from the ancient
Greek word *pepon*,
meaning
"ripe melon."

7

Nearly
half of Americans
say they
**believe in
ghosts,**
according to a
news poll.

8

Diners eat
surrounded by 22
occupied
graves
at a
restaurant
in
India.

9

Vampire bats
don't actually
suck blood—
they lap it up
with their tongues.

10

There's a
town called
**Frankenstein,
Missouri, U.S.A.**

159

Listen Up

for These Facts About
Sound

1

An **orchestra** in the Washington, D.C., area performs **only music** from **video games.**

2

A sound like **popping popcorn** is made by some **radio signals** coming from **Jupiter.**

4

Certain **sand dunes** occasionally **hum.**

3

A piece of music in Germany is being **played so slowly** it won't finish **until 2640.**

5

The **longest** recorded **echo** lasted for nearly **2 minutes.**

6

The Parma wallaby makes **coughing noises** to **communicate** with a **mate.**

7

In 2005, London began **playing classical music** in subway stations to **stop crime.**

8

The western diamondback **rattlesnake** can vibrate its rattle about **60 times a second.**

9

The **crack of a whip** is from the tip moving **so fast** it breaks the **sound barrier.**

10

Hot water and **cold** water make **different** sounds when **poured.**

BROWN VS. BLACK BEARS

Teddy bears make great picnic companions. Real bears? Not so much. The two main bears you'll find in the U.S. are black bears and brown bears, or grizzlies. They only share the same forests in a few places, like Yellowstone and Glacier National Parks. It's not as easy as the color of their coats! Black bears actually come in a range of colors (from white to brown to black), while grizzlies can be dark brown to blond. Instead, check out the bear's profile: a grizzly has a sort of hump between its shoulders, and a black bear has a bigger rump in the back. Another defining feature is the front claw: Black bears have short dark claws, and brown bears have longer white claws. But if you're close enough to see the claws, you're much too close!

162

What's the Difference?

MOTH VS. BUTTERFLY

To many people, moths are the ugly ducklings and butterflies are the beautiful swans. But why is that, when both winged creatures can be quite lovely? Perhaps the stereotype comes from the fact that butterflies (which emerge from a chrysalis) are generally more colorful than moths (born from cocoons). They also fly around during the day, while moths are nocturnal—like bats and raccoons. When a butterfly lands, it folds its wings together, as if it's trying to squeeze through a narrow space. Moths prefer to lie flat and stretch their wings out when they land. In the United States, there are about 18 times as many different kinds of moths than there are butterflies! With that much variety, there have to be some beauties among them, right?

CYCLONE VS. HURRICANE VS. TYPHOON

When a storm blows in 75-mile-an-hour (121-km/h) winds—faster than most cars drive down the highway—it's officially considered a hurricane, cyclone, or typhoon. But which name you use depends on where you are when that wind starts blowing. Hurricanes, cyclones, and typhoons are all rotating storms that form in the tropics. In the U.S., we're most familiar with hurricanes, which form in the Atlantic and northern Pacific Oceans. In the area of the Pacific that includes Japan, China, and the Philippines, those same storms are called typhoons. India and Bangladesh have cyclones, which form in the Bay of Bengal and Arabian Sea. Fun fact: In the Northern Hemisphere, these storms spin counterclockwise, and in the Southern Hemisphere, they spin clockwise. The direction doesn't seem to lessen the blow!

FRIES VS. CHIPS

Attention couch potatoes: A fry, a chip, and a crisp may be similarly fried bits of starchy tuber, but you'll get a different product depending on the country in which you're ordering! In the U.K., a chip is the standard name for what Americans call a french fry (though let's leave the French out of this entirely—they call them *frites*). But British chips tend to be thicker and more potato-y, and you'll most likely find them on a plate with fried fish. The sort of ultrathin, supersalty fries that are found at American fast-food chains have even caught on as "fries" in the U.K., since the American chains are also prevalent overseas. Confusing, huh? And if you find yourself at the Tower of London craving a bag of Ruffles, don't even think of calling them potato chips. In England, those are known as crisps! Po-TAY-to, po-TAH-to.

DARK CHOCOLATE VS. MILK CHOCOLATE VS. WHITE CHOCOLATE

It's shared on holidays, gobbled with delight, mixed into cookies, and whipped into mousse: It's chocolate, and more than seven million tons (6.4 million t) of it are eaten worldwide each year. But all chocolate is not created equal. Sure, it all starts with the cacao bean, which is picked, roasted, ground, and then separated into cocoa butter and cocoa powder—both important ingredients in chocolate. But dark chocolate is bitter because it has the most cocoa powder, ranging from 35 percent (mixed with cocoa butter and sugar) to 100 percent (not sweet at all, but good for baking). Milk chocolate—the base of most candy bars—has cocoa butter and cocoa powder, plus sugar and milk to make it creamy and delicious. White chocolate isn't technically chocolate at all! It's all sugar and cocoa butter and milk (and sometimes vanilla) and none of the brown cocoa powder that makes chocolate, chocolate.

FLOWER VS. WEED

One grows in your yard, the other ... also grows in your yard. What separates a flower and a weed? It may be as simple as whether you want it in your garden or not. Flowers are usually planted on purpose, enjoyed for their colorful displays and sweet-smelling blooms. Weeds are the pesky intruders that litter your yard and invade an otherwise perfect lawn. They can be quick-spreading but harmless (like crabgrass) or aggressive and threatening to the native plants in the area (like honeysuckle). Weeds can even have flowers—just look at the dandelions that pop up unwanted around the neighborhood. Picked flowers make beautiful bouquets, but picked weeds can be useful too—people eat several varieties, including dandelion greens and mint!

1

Every dolphin has a **signature whistle** it uses to identify itself.

2

Narwhals, which are part of the dolphin family, **look similar** to other species, except they have a **long ivory tusk like a unicorn.**

3

The word "porpoise" comes from an Old French word meaning "**pork fish.**"

4

When dolphins **get hurt,** they **heal more quickly** than other large sea creatures—**researchers** want to figure out how so they can **help humans.**

5

A California company builds expensive **dolphin-shaped boats** you can ride in to **do tricks** in the water.

6

A **pink** bottlenose dolphin was discovered in a Louisiana, U.S.A., lake.

7

Some **wild dolphins** play catch with **coconuts.**

8

To **stay alert** for predators, only half of a dolphin's brain goes to sleep.

Dolphin

Facts to
Flip Over

9
Newborn dolphins have a tiny patch of hair on their chins.

10
Risso's dolphins can **hold their breath** for 30 minutes.

Bottlenose dolphins

Tardigrade

1
When a
water drop
hits a puddle,
it **bounces** like a ball
until it's absorbed.

2
Earth's air
contains tiny bits of
diamonds
from space.

3
A **sneeze**
shoots out more than
40,000 particles
from the nose
and mouth.

4
Light can travel
a million times
faster
than a bullet.

Ultracool Facts About the Unseen World

5

A microscopic animal called the **tardigrade** can survive temperatures as low as minus 328°F (-200°C).

6

Birds see colors **invisible** to humans.

7

Each **gecko foot** has half a million tiny bristles for gripping surfaces such as walls.

8

Microbes were around before the dinosaurs.

9

People with **blond hair** generally have about 140,000 hair follicles, more than people with other hair colors.

10

A group of scientists estimated that there are seven quintillion, five hundred quadrillion **grains of sand** on the planet.

Facts About Plants to Grow Your Brain

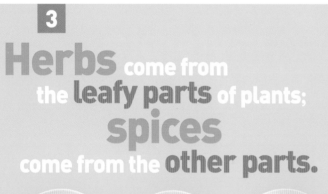

1

The seedpods of some snapdragon plants can **look like human skulls.**

2

One kind of **eucalyptus** tree can have **rainbow-colored bark.**

3

Herbs come from the **leafy parts** of plants; **spices** come from the **other parts.**

4

Attenborough's pitcher plant **secretes nectar** to **lure bugs** and rodents into its "mouth."

5 A Namibian *Welwitschia mirabilis* plant can **survive years without rain.**

6 Medicine made with certain **passionflowers** is used to help people **sleep.**

7 **Leaves** of a species of mimosa plant **curl** when touched.

8 The Yemen island of Socotra is home to **800 species** of plants, some believed to be **20 million years old.**

9 There are 50,000 edible plant species in the world, but three—**rice, maize** (corn), and **wheat**—make up more than half the world's food supply.

10 A common **sunflower's** main head consists of up to **4,000 tiny flowers.**

Mind-Bending

Facts About

the Brain

3 Pressing your tongue to the roof of your mouth eases "brain freeze."

6 It's impossible to tickle yourself because a part of your brain predicts the movement.

2 Exercise can make your brain more active.

5 Scientists don't fully understand why people yawn, but they believe the extra air cools off warm brains.

1 Your brain generates enough electricity to power a lightbulb.

4 Each minute, about three cups (750 mL), or two soda cans, of blood travel through the brain.

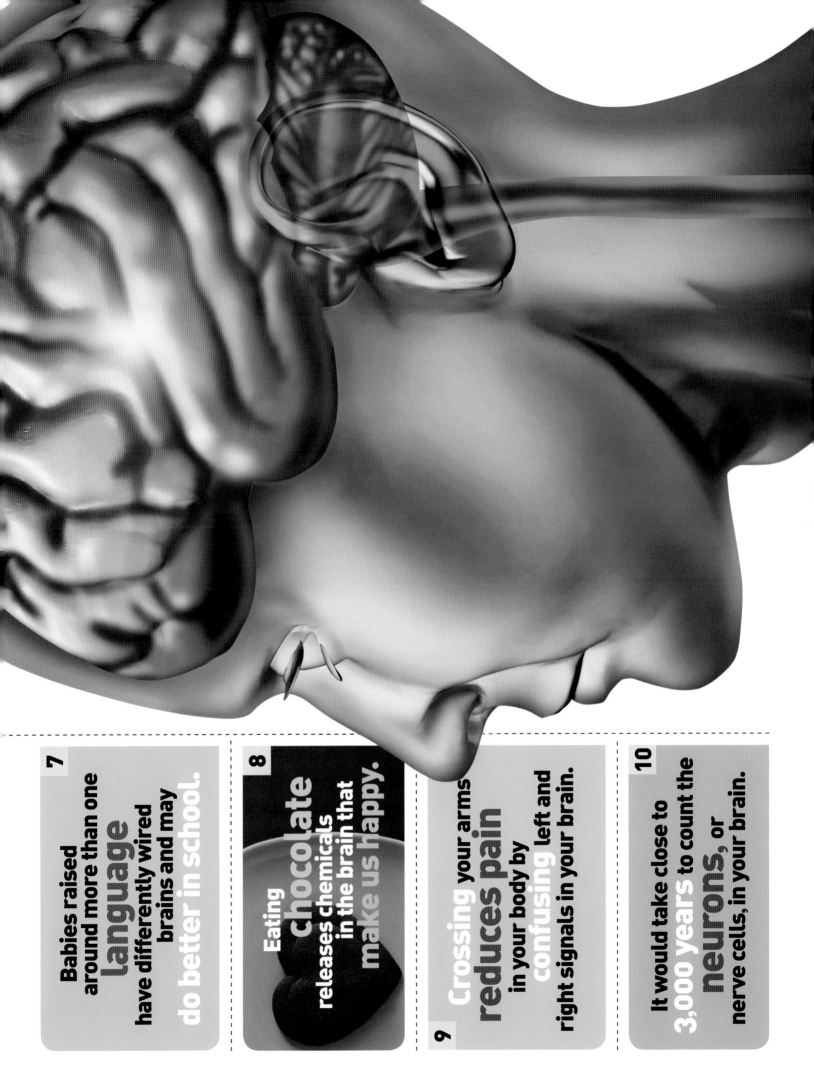

7

Babies raised around more than one **language** have differently wired brains and may **do better in school.**

8

Eating **chocolate** releases chemicals in the brain that **make us happy.**

9

Crossing your arms reduces pain in your body by **confusing** left and right signals in your brain.

10

It would take close to **3,000 years** to count the **neurons,** or nerve cells, in your brain.

1
The **ozone hole** over Antarctica is **larger** than **North America.**

2
Antarctica was located **near the Equator** hundreds of millions of years ago.

3
Most fish in Antarctica have natural "antifreeze" in their blood.

4
There are about **70 lakes** hidden **under Antarctic ice.**

5
It hasn't **rained** for at least **800,000 years** in parts of Antarctica.

6
Some penguins can dive **1,000 feet** (304.8 m) deep— that's about **150 times deeper** than an Olympic-size swimming pool.

7
One **giant iceberg** in Antarctica was nearly the size of Connecticut.

8
Wind gusts can blow more than **200 miles an hour** (322 km/h)—about as fast as a **race car's** top speed.

9
An **iceberg** in Antarctica looks like it's **bleeding,** but it's only leaking an **iron-rich liquid** that turns red in the air.

10
No dogs are allowed in Antarctica.

Antarctic
Facts That Will Give You the
Chills

Some sea cucumbers shoot out sticky threads to entangle or poison enemies.

Sense-ational Facts

1 Catfish use their **entire bodies** to taste things.

2 An elephant may **smell the air** by raising its trunk like a submarine **periscope.**

3  **Seahorses** can look in **two different directions** at once.

4 Certain **penguins** like the smell of **rotting cabbage.**

5 When the **Thirty Meter Telescope** is complete, it will be **5,000 times** more powerful than the **human eye,** making it the world's most powerful telescope.

6 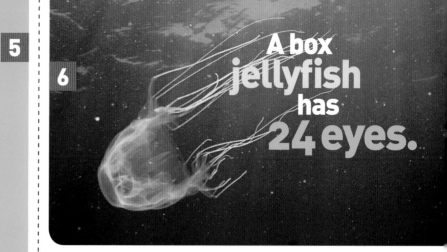 A box **jellyfish has 24 eyes.**

7 The same **taste cells** that detect sourness **also sense fizz.**

8 **Eighty percent** of what you think is taste is **actually smell.**

9 Some **flies can hear** each other land on a blade of grass.

10 **Monarch butterflies** have a kind of **internal GPS** that helps them migrate about **2,000 miles** (3,219 km) each year, always to the same location.

Frog
Facts to Jump Into!

1

Two frogs were married in India at a traditional ceremony attended by **2,000 guests.**

2

A species of frog in Borneo **oozes yellow goo** if you **pick it up.**

3

A chorus of **frog calls** can be heard more than **a mile away.** (1.6 km)

4

Frogs have been found in 25-million-year-old fossilized tree resin called **amber.**

5

A bullfrog named **Rosie the Ribiter** traveled more than **21 feet** (6.4 m) **in 3 hops.**

European tree frog

Marsh frog

6

Kermit
wasn't originally a frog—
he was a
lizardlike creature.

7

It **rained frogs** in
Kansas City, Missouri, U.S.A., after
strong winds sucked up
the animals and then
dropped them
from the sky.

8

Some frogs can **leap**
more than **20 times** their
body length.

9

One golden
poison
dart frog has
enough
toxin to kill
20,000 mice.

10

Certain frogs
can produce
more than
200,000
eggs in a
lifetime.

179

Incredible Facts About Ancient Egypt

1
Tombs were stocked with everything from food to chariots for use in the afterlife.

2
King Tut had four miniature coffins to hold his internal organs.

3
Egyptian doctors often **used honey** to treat patients.

4
The Egyptian **alphabet** contained more than 700 hieroglyphs.

6

Cleopatra, who ruled Egypt for about 22 years, was actually **Greek.**

8

Egyptians played a **sport** similar to baseball called tipcat.

10

Unwrapped, a mummy's bandages could stretch for half a mile. (0.8 km)

5

Egyptian people **worshipped** more than **2,000** gods and goddesses.

7

Pharaohs wore **fake beards** made of goat hair.

9

The **Great Pyramid** at Giza **weighs** as much as 16 Empire State Buildings.

Behind the Facts

W e're sure you're wondering how we got **so many awesome facts** about **so many awesome topics** into this book. First, we came up with a list of all the **coolest** and **most interesting** things out there—things we know kids want to know more about. Like **creepy-crawly critters** and mummies. Food, castles, and sharks. Ice cream. Treasures. Caves. **All kinds of stuff.** Then we found 10 or 20 of the most **exciting** and **surprising** facts about those topics to arrange on each page. We **carefully researched** each and every fact to make sure it's **absolutely true ...** and then we packed it full of **cool bonus content!** Things like ... strange places, moments of extreme weirdness around the world, and "What's the difference?" which will **answer age-old questions** like "what's the difference between an alligator and a crocodile?" And we illustrated and designed the pages so well that **you'll never get bored** looking at them and will love flipping to all your favorite parts. Bet you didn't know who worked to make this book—it took a group of **writers, editors, photo editors,** and **designers**—the greatest book team around!

Illustrations Credits

Index

Boldface indicates illustrations.

A

Abdullah II, King (Jordan) 95

Aboriginals, Australian 91

Acorns 99

Acrotholus audeti **12–13**

Africa 122–123, **122–123**

    languages 104, 122

    mythology 11

    primates 127

    yams 14

African elephants 25, **25**

Agra, India: marathon runner 55, **55**

Aircraft 56, **56,** 57, 121, **121**

Alaska, U.S.A.

    ice phone booth 111, **111**

    see also Anchorage; Talkeetna

Alkali bees 102

Alligators 41, 69, **69,** 141, **141**

Alster River, Germany 157, **157**

Amazon River, South America 73

Amber 178

Anchorage, Alaska, U.S.A.: outhouse race 55, **55**

Andes Mountains, South America 141, 143

Antarctica 68, 110, **110,** 172–173, **172–173**

    insect 97

    mummies 84

    summer daylight 139

    weather 16, 65, 173

Antelopes 130

Ants 51, 90, 96, 107, **107**

Apes 37, 127, **127**

Apollo 8 (spacecraft) 105

April Fool's Day 153

Arctic regions 68

Arctic terns 119

Argentina 69

Ascot, England: breakfast hat 157, **157**

Asia 14, 26, 65, 122, 127

Asian palm civets 117, **117**

Astrology 14

Astronauts 33, 77, 83, 93, 128, **128**

Astronomy 14

Athens, Georgia, U.S.A. 19

Atlantic Ocean 65, 73

Atlas moths 97, **97**

Attenborough's pitcher plants 168

Australia

    Aboriginals 91

    cave paintings 108

    dining 116

    heart-shaped reef 82, **82–83**

    marsupials 89

    rugby 69

    spiders 147

    see also Blue Mountains; Great Barrier Reef; Sydney

Avalanches 53

Avocados 44

Aztec 90

B

Baboons 85, 127

Bacteria 22, 35

Baldness 103

Balloons 56, **56,** 144

Bangladesh 163

Barbers 132

Baron Samedi (voodoo god) 10

Baseballs 29, **29,** 56, **56**

Basenjis 44

Bat bones 59

Bats 118, **118,** 141, 150–151, **150–151,** 159, 163

Battery, potato 86, **86**

Beards 75, **75,** 129, 181

Bears

    coat colors 162

    sense of smell 118

    see also Black bears; Brown bears; Polar bears

Beehive State 103

Bees 102–103, **102–103,** 139

Beetles 97, 155, **155**

Beijing, China

    fried scorpions 116, **116**

    giant unicycle 156, **156**

Bellatrix Lestrange (character) 6

Belly buttons 35

Bengal tigers 130, **130**

Berlin, Germany: panda sculptures 54, **54**

Bhut jolokia peppers 117, **117**

Bhutan 47

Bigfoot 19

Bighorn rams 140, **140–141**

Birds 60, 127, 167

    Arctic terns 119

    "barking pigeon" 40

    cassowaries 25, **25**

    chickens 137, **137**

    flamingos 141

    indigo buntings 7, **7**

    Pacific parakeets 140

    scarlet ibises 63, **63**

    song sparrows 57

    swans 157, **157**

    see also Penguins

Black bears 118, 162

Black light 96, 136

Black mambas 97, **97**

Black widow spiders 25, **25,** 147, **147**

Blarney Castle, Ireland 133

Blinking 36

Blonde hair 167

Blue Mountains, Australia: tree discovery 73

Blue whales 134, **134–135,** 148

Board games

    ancient Egypt 91

    see also Monopoly

Bogotá, Colombia: art installation 107, **107**

Bonaparte, Napoleon 70

Bonfires 105

Books 46–47, **46–47,** 55, **55**

Borborygmus 86

Borneo 178

Bottlenose dolphins 164, **164–165**

Box jellyfish 177, **177**

Brachiosaurus 30, **30–31**

Brain, human 35, 36, 170–171, **170–171**

Brain freeze 170

Brain-shaped phone booth 157, **157**

British Columbia, Canada 49, 73

Brontophobia 16

Brown bears 162, **162**

Brush-tailed bettongs 89

Bulgaria 58

Bullfrogs 56, 178

Bulls 63, **63**

Bumblebee bats 118, **118**

Butterflies 23, **23,** 72, **72,** 127, 163, 177, **177**

C

Cacao beans 90

California, U.S.A.: Ferris wheel **138–139,** 139

Caligula (Roman emperor) 90

Cambodia 49

Camels 29, **29, 94,** 122, **122**

Camouflage 130, 149

Canada

    one-million-dollar coin 39

    soccer 69

    see also British Columbia; Saskatchewan; Vancouver

Candy bars 48, 66, **66,** 79, **79,** 163

Candy corn 158, **158**

Candy hearts 83, **83,** 120, **120**

Canyons **94,** 95, 126, **126,** 143

Capybaras 73, **73**

Carrots 36, **36,** 50, **50,** 51

Cassava 117, **117**

Cassowaries 25, **25**

Castles 132–133, **132–133**

Catfish 176, **176**

Catnip 144

Cats 144–145, **144–145**

    ancient Egypt 85, 145

    mummies 85, **85**

    night vision 131

    urine 136

    wild cats 130–131, **130–131**

    see also Kittens

Cave bears 108

Cave paintings 108

Caves 108–109, **108–109,** 150

Chameleons 20, **20–21,** 119, **119**

Changsa, China: haircuts 107, **107**

Cheese **50–51,** 51

Cheetahs 82, **82,** 100, 131, **131**

Cherries 46, **46,** 69

Cherry pie **48–49,** 49

Chewing gum 87, **87,** 91

Chickens 137, **137**

Chihuahuas 44

Chimney sweeps 59

Chimpanzees 127

China

    beliefs 26

    good luck 58, 61

    terra-cotta army 98, **98**

    typhoons 163

    see also Beijing; Changsa; Great Wall of China; Xi'an

China, ancient 22, 91

Chionophobia 53

Chiroptophobia 151

Chocolate 44, 66–67, **66–67,** 76, 127, 163, **163,** 171

Chocolate bars 67, **67,** 76

Chocolate chip cookies 14, **14,** 66, **66**

Chocolates 66, **66,** 153

Christmas 105, 152, 153

Chromophobia 21

Cicadas 97

Cleopatra, Queen (Egypt) 70, 181, **181**

Clocks 39, **39**

Clouds 87, **87**

Clovers, four-leaf 59, **59**

Cockroaches 40, **40,** 149

Coconuts 164, **164**

Coffee 28, **28,** 117

Coffins 137, 159

Coins 38, **38,** 39, **39**

Colca Canyon, Peru 143

Color blindness 22, 63

Colors 20–23, **20–23,** 138, 167; *see also* Red

Colossal squid 119

Comb, giant 107, **107**

Communication, animal

    apes 127

    cats 144, 145

    dolphins 69

    gerbils 112

Confetti 18, **18**

Connecticut, U.S.A. 18

Constellations 6, 26

Cookie: word origin 77

Cookies

    chocolate chip 14, **14,** 66, **66**

    fortune 49, **49**

    macarons 127, **127**

Coolidge, Calvin 129

Coral reefs 65, **65,** 82, **82–83**

Cornflakes 98, **98**

Cotton candy 48, **48**

Cotton Castle, Denizli Province, Turkey 42–43, **42–43**

Cougars 131

Cows 8

Crab Nebula 92

Crab spiders 147, **147**

Crabs 63

Craters 126

Crayons **20,** 22, 63, **63**

Crocodiles

    mummified 122, **122**

    vs. alligators 69

    see also Nile crocodiles; Saltwater crocodiles

Crowns 99, **99**

Cucula (asteroid) 92

Curiosity (Mars rover) **32–33**

Cuvier's beaked whales 149

Cyclones 163

Cyclops (mythical creature) 10, **10–11**

D

D River, Oregon, U.S.A. 65

Dalmatians 44, 45, **45**

Death Valley, California, U.S.A. 65

Dentists 132

Desserts 76–77, **76–77**

Diamonds 21, 45, **86–87,** 87, 166

Dinosaurs 12–13, **12–13,** 26, 30, **30–31,** 75, **75,** 100

Diorama, city 106, **106**

Dogs 44–45, **44–45,** 144

    banned from Antarctica 173

    grass sculpture 157, **157**

    popular name 60

    White House pets 128

    see also Puppies

Dolphins 69, **69,** 164–165, **164–165**

Dorothy (character) 46

Doughnuts 77, **77,** 104, **104**

Draco (constellation) 26

Dragonflies 154, **154**

Dragons 26–27, **26–27**

Dreaming 35

Drupes 69

E

Earth

    atmosphere 100

    core 101

    ice ages 111

    surface 43, 65, 126

    tectonic plates 43, 126

    temperature 65, 100

    water 149

Earthquakes 42, 108

Echo, longest recorded 160

Echolocation 69

Eels 50, **50**

Eggs

    ants 51

    black widow spiders 25

    dinosaurs 13

    dragons 26

    as food **47,** 120, **120,** 157

    frogs 179

    ocean sunfish 114

    termites 97

Egypt, ancient 180–181, **180–181**

    beliefs 83

    board games 91

    cats 85, 145

        mummies 85, 85, 91, 122, 122, 137, 181

El Castillo, Chichén Itza, Mexico **90–91**

Elephants 25, **25,** 41, 115, **115,** 176, **176**

Elizabeth II, Queen (United Kingdom) 71, **71,** 99

Emperor penguins 2, **2–3**

Empire State Building, New York, New York, U.S.A. **149**

England 22, 27, 61, 163; *see also* Ascot; Liverpool; London; Windsor Castle

Ethiopia 123

Eucalyptus trees 168, **168**

European shrews 25

European tree frogs **178**

Exercise 170

Eye colors 21, 145

Eyeballs 35

Eyebrows 35, 154

Eyelashes 35

F

Fairy floss 48, **48**

False teeth 128

Families, animal 24–25, **24–25,** 69

Fast-food chains 22

Faucet, floating 157, **157**

Feet, animal

    geckos 167

    gerbils 112

    rabbits 61

Feet, human 36, 154

Felix the Cat (character) 144

Ferris wheels **138–139,** 139

Fingernails 36

Fingerprints 35, 41, 44

Fingers, crossing 59, **59**

Fire trucks 80–81, **80–81**

Fireflies 155

Fires 105, 109

Fireworks 139, **139**

Fish, cave-dwelling 109

Flamingos 141

Flat rock scorpions **96–97**

Flies 97, 154, 177, **177**

Flowers

    bees and 102, **102–103**

    "corpse flower" 136, **136**

    passionflowers 169, **169**

    snapdragons 168, **168**

    sunflowers 169, **169**

    tulips 43, **43**

    vs. weeds 163

    world's biggest 73

Flying lizards **56–57,** 57

Football, American 69

Football, world's oldest 133

Ford, Gerald R. 129

Fortune cookies 49, **49**

Fossils 147, **147,** 178

France 85, 96, 127; *see also* Lille; Lyon

Frankenstein, Missouri, U.S.A. 159

French fries 163, **163**

Fried chicken 152, **152**

Frogs 17, 155, 178–179, **178–179**; *see also* Poison dart frogs

Frozen pops 22, **22**

Fruit preserves 127, **127**

Fruit soup 117

Fruitadens 75

Fruitcakes 105, **105**

Fruits: rain forest 73

G

Galaxies 6

Gandhi, Mohandas 70, **70**

Garderobes 132, **132**

Garfield, James 129

Geckos 167

Genes 86

Gentoo penguins 118, **118**

George, Saint 27

Gerbils 112, **112**

Germany 59, 160; *see also* Berlin; Hamburg; Neuschwanstein Castle

Ghost bats 150

Ghosts 11, 136, **136,** 158, 159, **159**

Giant prickly stick insects 96

Giant squid 14, 40

Giant water bugs 155

Gingerbread houses 105, **105**

Giraffes, wild 118

Glaciers 87, 110

Glass, breaking 58

Glazed doughnuts 77, **77**

Gold nuggets 99, **99**

Golden hamsters 113, **113**

Golden poison dart frogs 179, **179**

Golden silk orb-weavers 146, **146**

Goldstein, Paul 55, **55**

Goosebumps (book series) 47

Grand Canyon, Arizona, U.S.A. 126, **126**

Grant, Ulysses S. 129

Grapes 44, 58, **58**

Grasshoppers 73, **73**

Great Barrier Reef, Australia 65, **65**

Great Pyramid, Giza, Egypt 181, **181**

Great Wall of China, China 64, **64–65**

Great white sharks 125, **125**

Greece 59, 61

Greek (language) 23, 95, 159

Greek mythology 10

Greeks, ancient 103

Green Eggs and Ham (Dr. Suess) 47

Greenland shark meat 124

Grizzly bears 162, **162**

Guano 151

Guinea pigs 112, **112,** 116

H

Hailstones 16, **16**

Hair, human 17, 35, 63, 167

Haircuts, weird 107, **107**

Halloween 107, **107,** 158–159, **158–159**

Ham 99, **99**

Hamamatsu, Japan: grass dog 157, **157**

Hamburg, Germany: swan roundup 157, **157**

Hamburgers **16, 79**

Handbags, designer 76

Hanukkah 104, 152

Harry Potter books 6, 47, 71

Hats 157, **157**

Hawks: mummies **84–85,** 85

Hazelnuts 69

Hearts 35, 36, 57, 82–83, **82–83,** 87, 134

Herbs 168, **168**

Hershey's Kisses 67, **67**

Hibernacula 150

Hierapolis, Turkey 43

Higgins, Michael D. 70

Hippo tusks 128

Hives, bee 103, **103**

Holidays 104–105, 152–153

Honey 103, **103,** 180, **180**

Honeybees 103, **103**

Horse-drawn carriages 129

Horses 19, **19,** 47, **47,** 58, **58,** 90, 141

Horseshoes 60, **60**

Hot Coffee, Mississippi, U.S.A. 28

Hot springs **42,** 43, 108

Houseflies 154

Human body 34–37, **34–37;** *see also* Brain, human

Hurricanes 163, **163**

I

Ice ages 111

Ice caves 108

Ice cream 8–9, **8–9,** 77

Ice-cream floats 75, **75**

Ice cubes 110, **110**

Ice phone booth 111, **111**

Ice skates 111, **111**

Icebergs 100, 110, 111, 172, **172–173,** 173

Iceland

    dining 116, 124

    glaciers 87

    hot springs 108

    ice caves 108

    mythology 11

    volcanoes 87

Igloos 75, **75**

Illinois, U.S.A. 98

Inca 111, 143

India

    ancient surgeons 90

cyclones 163

    frog wedding 178, **178**

    national animal 130

    peppers 117, **117**

    restaurant 159

    see also Agra

Indian Ocean 87

Indigo buntings 7, **7**

Indonesia 73, 152

Italy 58, 96, 153

J

Jaguars 141

Jam 127, **127**

James and the Giant Peach (Dahl) 46, **46**

Japan

    fortune cookies 49

    holidays 152, 153

    myths 10

    typhoons 153

    underwater mailbox 149

    see also Hamamatsu; Shibuya; Tokyo

Japanese (language) 46

Jell-O 77

Jelly 49, **49,** 127, **127**

Jelly beans 128

Jelly-filled doughnuts 104, **104**

Jellyfish 114, 138, **138,** 177, **177**

Jet aircraft 121, **121**

Joan of Arc **70–71,** 71

Jordan

    ancient city **94,** 95, **95**

    national dish 95

Jupiter (planet) 100, 160

K

Kamehameha I, King (Hawaiian Islands) 71

Kangaroos 41, 88, **88,** 116

Kansas City, Missouri, U.S.A. 179

Kentucky Fried Chicken 152

Kermit (character) 179, **179**

Ketchup 70, **70**

King cakes 60, **60**

Kites 57, **57**

Kittens 120, **120,** 144, **144,** 145, **145**

Kitti's hog-nosed bats 150

Koi fish 121

Komodo dragons 74, **74**

Kwanzaa 104

L

Ladybugs 58, **58**

Laughing 36

Laundry 18, **18**

Leafy seadragons 149, **149**

Lego bricks 121, **121**

Legumes 69; *see also* Peanuts

Lemons 49, 138, **138**

Leopard seals 68

Leopards 130

Lesser horseshoe bats **151**

Li Yongli 156, **156**

Library of Congress, Washington, D.C., U.S.A. 47

Lice 111

Light 7, 138–139, **138–139,** 166

Lightbulbs 138, 170, **170**

Lighthouses 138

Lightning 29, **29,** 93, 100, 139, **139**

Lille, France: street market 107, **107**

Lincoln, Abraham 129

Lions **122–123,** 123, **131,** 144

Lion's mane jellyfish 114

Little brown bats **150–151**

Liverpool, England: sculptures **107**

Lobsters 137, **137**

London, England: classical music 161

Louisiana, U.S.A. 164

Lyon, France: inflatable mouse 107, **107**

M

Macaroni and cheese **22**

Macarons 127, **127**

Macaroons 127

Machu Picchu, Peru **142,** 143

Madrid, Spain: book tower 55, **55**

Mailbox, underwater 149

Malaysian flying foxes 150

Mamenchisaurus 12

Manatees **114–115,** 115

Marathons 55

Mars (planet) 32–33, **32–33,** 93, 126

Mars (Roman god) 33, **33**

Marsh frogs **179**

Marshmallows 14, 76, **76**

Marsupials 88–89, **88–89**; *see also* Kangaroos

Maya 70, 91

Medicine and health 45, 49, 90, 91, 108, 169, 180

Meerkats 24, **24–25**

Mekong River, Southeast Asia 10

Melons 153, **153**

Menorahs 104, **104,** 152, **152**

Mexico 51, 99; *see also* El Castillo; Oaxaca; Piedras Negras

Miami Beach, Florida, U.S.A. 19

Mice 99, **99,** 113; *see also* Northern grasshopper mice

Microbes 167

Micropachycephalosaurus 13

Microraptor 12

Microwave ovens 78, **78**

Milk 8, 137, **137,** 163

Milky Way (galaxy) 6

Mimosa plant 169

Minnesota, U.S.A. 50

Mir space station 77

Mites 136, **136,** 154

Mobile, Alabama, U.S.A. 18

Mobula rays 140

Moctezuma (Aztec ruler) 67

Moles 61

Monarch butterflies 177, **177**

Monarchs 69

Money 38–39, **38–39,** 90

Monkeys 127, 140, **140**

Monopoly (game)

    fake money 39

    houses 21, **21**

Montana, U.S.A. 18

Moon 14, 92, **92,** 100, 105, **105,** 128

Moonbows 16

Morocco 123

Morpho achilles 72, **72**

Moscow, Russia **62,** 106, **106**

Mosquitoes 151, 154

Moths 97, **97,** 163, **163**

Mountain lions 131

Mountains, tallest 65

Mummies 84–85, **84–85,** 122, **122,** 137, 181

Music 160, 161

Mustangs 141

N

Nabateans 95

Nachos 50, **50**

Naga fireballs 10

Naked mole rats 113, **113**

Narwhals 68, 164, **164**

National Parfait Day 77

Neapolitan mastiff 45

Nectar 102, 103, 168

Neptune (planet) 86, **86,** 92, 93

Neurons 171

Neuschwanstein Castle, Germany 132, **132–133**

Neutron stars 7

New Caledonia, South Pacific Ocean 83

New Mexico, U.S.A. 98

New Orleans, Louisiana, U.S.A.: king cakes 60, **60**

New Year celebrations 58, 61, 139, **139**

New York, New York, U.S.A.: menorah 153, **153**

Nicaragua 140

Nile crocodiles 25

Nile River, Africa 65, **65**

Nixon, Richard M. 70, 128

Nocturnal animals 163

Northern grasshopper mice 141

Nostradamus 15

Numbats 89

Nuts 16, 69

O

Oaxaca, Mexico 153
Obama, Barack 71, 129
Observatories, astronomical 143
Ocean sunfish 114
Octopuses 14, 82, **82**, 114, **114,** 127
Odysseus (legendary hero) **10–11**
Olive oil ice cream 77
Oranges 22, **27,** 78, **78**
Orcas 114, **114**
Oscar the Grouch (character) 21
Outhouse race 55, **55**
Oxyuranus microlepidotus 119
Ozone hole 172

P

Pacific Ocean 65, 163
Pacific parakeets 140
Pademelons 88, **88**
Pallid bats 150
Palm Islands, Dubai, United Arab
    Emirates 75, **75**
Pamukkale, Denizli Province, Turkey
    42–43, **42–43**
Panda sculptures 54, **54**
Panthers 131
Parachute jumps 56
Paradise, Tom 95
Parma wallabies 161, **161**
Passionflowers 169, **169**
Passports 71, 85, **85**
Pasta 50
Peaches 10, **10,** 69
Peanut butter 49, **49,** 96, 116, **116**
Peanuts 49, 69, **69**
Pearls 99, **99**
Penguins **2–3,** 25, 68, 118, **118,** 172, **172,**
    176, **176**
Pennies 38, **38,** 39, **39**
Peppers 63, **63,** 117, **117**
Percy Jackson and the Olympians
    (Riordan) 47
Perfume 70, **70**
Perspiration 102
Peru

dining 116
good luck 61
rain forests 73, 143
see also Colca Canyon; Machu
    Picchu; Puruchuco
Petra, Jordan **94,** 95, **95**
Pets
    Halloween costumes **158–159,** 159
    holiday gifts 105
    special airline 56
    see also Cats; Dogs
Pharaohs 181
Phasmaphobia 136
Phone booths
    brain-shaped 157, **157**
    made of ice 111, **111**
Pi (number) 120
Pickles 18, **18**
Piecaken 117
Piedras Negras, Mexico 50
Pies **48–49,** 49, 76, **76,** 117
Pigs 19, **19,** 29, **29,** 58, 99
Pineapple 70, 155
Pirates 98, **98**
Pizza 51, 78, **78**
Plants 168–169, **168–169;** *see also*
    Flowers
Pocatello, Idaho, U.S.A. 19
Poe, Edgar Allan 75
Poison 117, 119, 127
Poison dart frogs 24, **24, 127,** 179, **179**
Poland 117, 143
Polar bears 68, **68,** 118, **118**
Poop, animal 86; *see also* Guano
Popcorn 108, 160, **160–161**
Porpoise: word origin 164
Porpoises 69
Portugal 96
Postcards 149
Potato chips 163; *see also* Pringles
Potatoes 50, 79, 86, **86,** 93; *see also*
    French fries; Potato chips
Praying mantises **154–155,** 155
Presidents, U.S. 69, 70, 71, 128–129
Primates 127, **127**
Pringles 117, 117

Pufferfish 127
Puffins 116, **116**
Pumas 131
Pumpkins **158–159,** 159
Puppies 44, 45, 120, **120**
Purple: word origin 22
Puruchuco (site), Peru 85
Pyramids **90–91,** 122, **122, 145,** 181, **181**

Q

Quechua (language) 143

R

Rabbits **60–61,** 61
Raccoons 129, **129,** 163
Race cars 55, **55**
Radio signals 160
Radishes 153, **153**
Rain forests 72–73, **72–73,** 143
Raindrops 16
Rats 112, 113, **113**
Reagan, Ronald 128
Red (color) 62–63, **62–63**
Red hair 63, **63**
Red kangaroos 88
Red peppers 63, **63,** 117, **117**
Red Sea 62
Reef squid **15**
Reinhard, Johan 143
Risso's dolphins 165
Roadkill 18
Rock candy 49, **49**
Rock salt 9
Rodents 112–113, **112–113,** 168; *see also*
    Capybaras; Guinea pigs; Mice
Roman Empire 43, 95
Rome, ancient 22
Roosevelt, Franklin D. 128
Rowling, J. K. 47
Rubies 62,
Rugby 69
Russian (language) 62

S

Sahara desert, Africa 122

Saliva 35, 112

Salt 9, 39, **39,** 121, **121**

Saltwater crocodiles 119, **119**

San Francisco, California, U.S.A. 18

Sand, grains of 167

Sand dunes 123, 160, **160**

Sandboarding 123, **123**

Sandwiches

    grilled cheese 74

    peanut butter-and-jelly 49, **49,** 127

Santa Claus 104, 153, **153**

Saskatchewan, Canada: snowball fight 52

Saturn (planet) 93, **93**

Scarlet ibises 63, **63**

Scatologists 86

Schnoodles 44

Scorpions 96, **96–97,** 116, **116,** 127, 150

Scuba divers 149

Sea cucumbers **174–175,** 175

Sea otters 114, **114**

Sea stars 40, **40**

Sea turtles 40, **40–41**

Seahorses 114, 176, **176**

Seaweed 19, **19,** 49, **49,** 149

Sendak, Maurice 47

Senegal 22

Servals 131, **131**

Sharks 114, 124–125, **124–125**

Sheep 22, **22,** 118, **118**

Shellfish 22

Shibuya, Japan: crosswalk 121, **121**

Shortfin mako sharks 124, **124**

Silk, spider 146

Sirius (star) 17

Sirius Black (character) 6

Skamania County, Washington, U.S.A. 19

Sleep

    bees 102

    dolphins 164

    giraffes 118

    guinea pigs 112

Sleeping Beauty Castle, Disneyland, U.S.A. 132

Slugs 86, **86**

Smell, sense of

    bears 118

    big cats 131

Smith, David 56

Smoothies 111, **111**

S'mores 76, **76**

Snakes 10, 11, **11,** 97, **97,** 119, 161, **161**

Snapdragons 168, **168**

Sneezes 166

Snow 52–53, **52–53,** 110–111, **110–111**

Snow leopards 131, **131**

Soap 79, **79**

Soccer 69

Soccer ball, world's oldest 133

Socotra (island), Yemen 169

Soda 48, 116

Solstices 143

Song sparrows 57

South Korea 152

Space 92–93, **92–93**

Space travel 33, 56, 105

Spacecraft 33, 77, 93, 105, 138

Spain

    ant supercolony 96

    New Year's Eve 58

    southern coast 123

    unlucky date 61

    see also Madrid

Spices 95, 168, **168**

Spider-Man comic books 129

Spider monkeys 140, **140**

Spiders 146–147, **146–147**

    leg regrowth 155

    as sign of good luck 61

    smallest known 74

    venom 127

    see also Black widow spiders; Tarantulas

Spiny dogfish sharks 125

Spotted bats 151

Squid 14, **15,** 40, 119

Star Wars movies 122

Stars 6–7, **6–7,** 14, 29, 87, 92, **92–93**

Stegosaurus 12

Stevenson, Robert Louis 46

Stilt walkers 55, **55**

Stirling Castle, Scotland 133, **133**

Stomachs 86, 102, 125

Stop signs 63, **63**

Strawberries 49

Stubbs (cat) 145

Sugar gliders 89, **89**

Sun 14, 28, **28,** 138

Sunflowers 169, **169**

Sunglasses 10, 21, **21**

Supercells 16

Swahili (language) 104

Swans 157, **157**

Sweat bees 102

Sweden 152

Sweet potatoes 14, **14,** 15

Switzerland 112

Swordfish 148, **148–149**

Swords 132, **132**

Sydney, Australia: seaside sculptures 55, **55**

T

T. rex 12

Tadpoles 24, **24**

Taiwan 50

Talkeetna, Alaska, U.S.A.: cat mayor 145

Tambourines 102, **102**

Tanzania 123

Tapirs 24, **24**

Tarantulas 49, 146, **146**

Tardigrades **166–167,** 167

Tasmanian devils 88, **88**

Taste cells 177

Tea 91

Teeth, animal

    alligators 41

    ants 90

    dolphins 69

    porpoises 69

    rats 113

sharks 125, **125**

Teeth, human 34, **34,** 51, 99

Telescopes **7,** 14, 177

Termites 89, **89,** 97, 155

Terra-cotta army 98, **98**

Texas, U.S.A. 151

Thailand 10, 109

Thanksgiving 14, 50, 144

Thunder 16

Thunderstorms 16

Tiger costume 55, **55**

Tigers 130, **130,** 144, **144**

Toenails 36

Toilets, castle 132, **132**

Tokyo, Japan: stilt walkers 55, **55**

Tongue prints 35

Tornadoes 16, **16–17,** 17

Tortoises 127, **127,** 141

Trains, passenger 121

Trash 79, **79**

Treasure Island (Stevenson) 46, **46**

Treasure Island, California, U.S.A. 99

Treasures 98–99, **98–99**

Tree resin 178

Tree sap 91

Triskadekaphobia 60

Tube-lipped nectar bats 141

Tulips 43, **43**

Tunisia 122

Tunnels, secret 133

Turkey (country) 42, 43, 59; *see also* Cotton Castle

Turkmenistan 153

Turtles 17, 127; *see also* Sea turtles

Tutankhamun, King (Egypt) 180

Twinkies **76–77,** 77

Typhoons 163

U

Ultraviolet light 139

Umbrellas 10, **10**

Unicycle, giant 156, **156**

United States

flag 62, **62**

lightning 29

money 38, **38,** 39, **39**

odd laws 18–19

pets 105, 120, 144

presidents 69, 128–129

Uranus (planet) 92, 93

Urine, cat 136

U.S. Capitol, Washington, D.C., U.S.A. **14,** 15

U.S. Postal Service 104

Utah, U.S.A. 103, 108

V

Valentine's Day 153

Vampire bats 159

Vancouver, Canada: light display 107, **107**

Vatican City 74, **74**

Velociraptor 12

Venom 103, 127, 150

Venus (planet) 29, **29,** 126

VFTS 102 (star) 6

Video games 160

Vietnam 26

Vikings 10, 91

Virginia, U.S.A.: water-skiing Santa 153, **153**

Vitamin C 49

Volcano: word origin 100

Volcanoes 32, 87, 126, 140

Vulcan (Roman god) 100

VY Canis Majoris (star) 7

W

Wales

flag 26, **26**

good luck 58

Walruses 114, **114**

Warthogs 41, **41**

Washington, George 8, 45, 128

Water: hot vs. cold 28, 161

Water drops 166

Water tap, suspended 157, **157**

Waterspouts 17, **17**

Weather 16–17, **16–17**

Wedding dress, spider in 61

Weddings

frog wedding 178, **178**

inside bowl of pasta 50

Weeds 163

Welwitschia mirabilis 169

West Africa 61

Western diamondback rattlesnakes 161, **161**

Whale sharks 124, **124**

Whales 131, 134, **134–135,** 148, 149

Where the Wild Things Are (Sendak) 47

Whips 161, **161**

Whirligig beetles 155, **155**

White Day 153

White dwarf stars 6

White House, Washington, D.C., U.S.A. 128, **128–129,** 129, 158

Wildfires 109

Windsor Castle, England 133, **133**

Wingless fly 97

Wombats 89, **89**

The Wonderful Wizard of Oz (Baum) 46, **46**

Worms 96

X

Xi'an, China: dragon sculpture **26–27**

Y

Yachts 39, **39**

Yams 14, 15

Yawning 170, **170**

Yellow underwear 61, **61**

Ypres, Belgium: floating faucet 83, **83**

Z

Zebrafish 82, **82**

Zebras 41, **41**

Zombie stars 6

Since 1888, the National Geographic Society has funded more than 12,000 research, exploration, and preservation projects around the world. The Society receives funds from National Geographic Partners, LLC, funded in part by your purchase. A portion of the proceeds from this book supports this vital work. To learn more, visit natgeo.com/info.

NATIONAL GEOGRAPHIC and Yellow Border Design are trademarks of the National Geographic Society, used under license.

For more information, visit nationalgeographic.com, call 1-877-873-6846, or write to the following address:

National Geographic Partners
1145 17th Street N.W.
Washington, DC 20036-4688 U.S.A.

Visit us online at nationalgeographic.com/books

For librarians and teachers: ngchildrensbooks.org

More for kids from National Geographic: natgeokids.com

For information about special discounts for bulk purchases, please contact National Geographic Books Special Sales: specialsales@natgeo.com

For rights or permissions inquiries, please contact National Geographic Books Subsidiary Rights: bookrights@natgeo.com

Art directed by Callie Broaddus
Designed by James Hiscott, Jr., and Chad Tomlinson

Hardcover ISBN: 978-1-4263-2837-4
Reinforced library binding ISBN: 978-1-4263-2838-1

Printed in Hong Kong
20/PPHK/6

The publisher gratefully acknowledges everyone who worked to make this book come together: Becky Baines, project editor; Lori Epstein, photo editor; Chelsea Lin, writer; Perry Martin, fact-checker; Michaela Weglinski, editorial assistant; Gus Tello, design production assistant; Anne LeongSon, design production assistant; Sally Abbey, managing editor; Joan Gossett, editorial production manager; Molly Reid, production editor.